BRUNO BETTELHEIM, recognized throughout the world as one of the greatest living child psychologists, was born in Vienna in 1903. He received his doctorate at the University of Vienna, and in 1939, after a year in the concentration camps at Dachau and Buchenwald, he came to America. He is Distinguished Professor of Education and Professor of both psychology and psychiatry at the University of Chicago and has been widely honored, especially for his work with autistic children. He is the author of many celebrated books, among them are: THE CHILDREN OF THE DREAM*, DIALOGUES WITH MOTHERS*, LOVE IS NOT ENOUGH*, and THE INFORMED HEART*.

D0908024

*Available in Avon Discus editions

DIALOGUES
WITH
MOTHERS

BRUNO BETTELHEIM

 A DISCUS BOOK/PUBLISHED BY AVON BOOKS

AVON BOOKS
A division of
The Hearst Corporation
959 Eighth Avenue
New York, New York 10019

To Ruth, Naomi, and Eric

CONTENTS

Dialogues with Mothers

INTRODUCTION

Nowadays we want our children to make their own decisions, but *we expect those decisions to please us.*

Life was much easier for my parents: they knew what a child was supposed to do, and he had jolly well better do it. But things are different with us. We want our children to live according to their own lights, to develop their personalities in freedom. This we do because we believe in freedom and know that coercion is bad. At the same time, we want their development to lead to goals we have set for them. Fearful of spoiling their spontaneity and happiness, we refrain from imposing our wishes on them; yet we want to end up with the same results as though we had.

There is nothing new, of course, about parents wanting to do right by their child. What is new is that we have grown very afraid of doing wrong by our children. Yet, strange as it sounds, I have more often seen things go very wrong because of a parent's fear of erring than because he did the wrong thing out of honest conviction. I have also seen parents who would not follow their correct instincts because they feared it would be bad for the child.

It is not quite as simple as if parents had nothing to worry about but fear, or needed only to follow their instincts in dealing with their children. But modern American parents need very much to sort out in their minds how they see their own function as parents, and what they want for and from their children. To help in this task was the purpose of my dialogues, as it is also the purpose of this book. Parents cannot be told what to do, or how to do it. What does help is increasing clarification about what they want for their child, and how, in everyday practice, to make this desire, slow step by step, become reality.

I speak here as if parents share equally in raising their children. But, though more of the early load falls to the mother, this book is meant for fathers and mothers. Unless both parents share a common understanding of what they want for their children, and unless the father supports the mother in achieving those goals, she alone will not succeed in her efforts—though she carries much the heavier burden of work and, accordingly, knows the richer rewards for success when they come.

Thus my first readers may well be young mothers, who I trust will then share the book with their husbands. For the mothers, especially with the first child, parenthood is quite an upheaval in spite of the natural fulfillment. They have been made aware of how terribly important they are in the child's early life, but this very awareness often makes them uncertain about how they are doing.

In response to their anxiety, they are swamped with literature in which they are sometimes made out to be saints, sometimes vipers, but always persons bearing vast responsibility. This alone is unnerving to a woman who knows she is only an average human being. Yes, she wants to be a mother and enjoys it, but she did not count on the myriad of things she is told can go wrong with her child, all of which would be her doing. By contrast, taking care of her child is said to be simple, and in her everyday experience changing diapers is not very glamorous, whatever the consequence of how she does it may be. What is more, discussing children is looked upon as small talk. Somehow mothers feel a discrepancy between how important they look in the scientific papers on child development and the image of "just a housewife" that confronts them as often.

During my round-table talks with young mothers, they began to see and hear for themselves how others felt, and—encouraged by me, whom they considered an authority—they could admit to themselves that caring for a small child is not always wholly blissful and entails genuine hardship. It was a relief for them to learn that all mothers are sometimes exhausted from the labor of caring for babies, the home, and a husband distracted by the desire for professional advancement and the need for making ends meet.

My overt goal—that of changing some of the parents' fundamental attitudes toward themselves as parents, toward their children, and toward child rearing— was much more difficult. Basically they wanted a set of rules about What to Do and What Not to Do. Each mother wanted me to silence the inner voice that was critical of some things she was doing, or that of a critical mother or husband. It was hard educational work to convince them that what might be right for one mother and child wasn't necessarily best for another—that it wasn't that simple. Eventually they saw that to be oneself even with one's own child wasn't dangerous either.

At the same time, and without any conscious intent, the sessions removed the mothers' seemingly trivial problems from the level of small talk. It became clear in which way child rearing is a job that demands correct observation, reflection, and personal decision. These the sessions restored—both the right and the duty to make personal decisions and the training to do it. It made parenthood exciting again when it seemed to have deteriorated to a rote list of do's and don'ts. In time it was only natural that a heightened self-respect was the outcome. And this the book should also do for its readers.

All of which is still needed, though by now there is

13

no lack of theories, books of theory, or handbooks of advice on how to raise children. Yet parents continue to have difficulty. This is not because the theories are faulty or the advice incorrect; usually both advice and theory are fine for dealing with other people's children. The difficulty is that they give little help and create much confusion when a parent tries to use them as a basis for living with his own children. Because, while most of the theories are pretty sound and while the same is true for much of the advice parents get, somehow none of it quite fits.

In my work as a foster parent to some forty difficult youngsters at the Orthogenic School, and in my private experience as the father of three, I have had to learn the hard way what all other parents also discover: that the most appropriate advice, the most carefully explained theory, is of little use when it comes to handling specific everyday events with a child. The over-all theories are just too broad, or permit of too many different ways of application, to offer more than a guiding idea in an instance where a very specific action is needed. Where the advice is specific, it is usually so specific that it never quite fits the situation confronting one.

Moreover, the parent described in such recommendations is not quite the type of person any of us feels himself to be, and the child described in print is not quite the particular child with whom we must deal. After all, behind all our actions in a given situation is the whole of our past life experience, which soon begins to influence our view of what we are doing to our child and of what he is doing to us. The same is true for our child: he, too, reacts to our intervention in terms of his past experiences, many of which we ourselves have provided or shaped. Yet no advice can allow for all these considerations without becoming so general and vague as to say that we must act in terms of our own and the child's history and personality.

However true this may be, it does not tell us what we should actually do.

Every parent and educator knows this difficulty and tries to deal with the impasse somehow. To me it was a particularly burning problem, as it must be to anyone in charge of a children's institution, where the staff looks to him for both theory and advice on handling child behavior.

Having thus been confronted, day in and day out for nearly twenty years, with the problem of how to help others to solve the problems entailed in living with children, and having been forced to help them deal with the most difficult problems children can present to adults, I came to realize that no teaching of theories will do; nor will any instructions on what exactly to do in a specific situation. I had to learn that only those theories help that have come to be part of one's own life by the practice of years, in ever varying situations, and with an a priori unpredictable outcome. But how can a theory become part of one's life through practice when one has never been taught it? Very much, I'm afraid, in the way the Bourgeois Gentilhomme suddenly realized he had been talking prose all his life, long before he knew there was a distinction.

What I learned to practice with our staff was simply this: to start out with the valid assumption that in asking for help they were interested, not in any theory or advice, but in a way of living more at ease with the children in their care—and hence more at ease with themselves. Achieving this called for innumerable instances of investigating the child's possible motives for his actions. Nearly always this led to the realization that a behavior that appeared stupid or perverted made good sense when so analyzed. It then appeared that if a child stepped on one's toes, it was due neither to clumsiness nor cussedness, but was simply an effort to reach a specific goal.

Everybody, nowadays, subscribes to the conviction

15

that our children make good sense, even to their breaking of our bones. But there is a very long way indeed from this theoretical conviction to accepting the fact that a child's breaking of our bones makes good sense. Also, if it were as simple as that, it would seem to follow that he *should* break our bones—a conclusion that, I submit, is just as perverted an idea as their breaking of an adult's bones in a perverted action. Obviously then, the valid theory that our children make good sense can become a guide for action fraught with serious danger to the child and ourselves.

The general principle that we must find ways to live more successfully with our children (so that they will not break our bones or theirs) hence makes better sense than the valid theory that whatever they do they do for excellent reasons. More important, it provides a far more powerful motive for thinking about one's own motives, behavior, and attitudes. Only after one has experimented with ways of living more successfully with a difficult child—and has found out what helps and what hinders—does one see sense in those theories that present in a general way what one has been practicing all along. But by that time there is usually small need for the theories, except in explaining one's actions to others.

How, then, can one help other persons to live more successfully with their children?

The only teaching that has helped the staff of the Orthogenic School were the efforts, free of theory or advice, at getting them to analyze a particular situation in their own words, on the basis of their own anxieties, notions, and hopes. By meandering, so to speak, around the concrete situation, they learned how many seemingly disconnected thoughts and feelings had entered the situation. These were no prearranged situations, but simply those that arose out of everyday living.

In the beginning our staff members usually asked for advice on how to handle a particular situation or wondered what theory should underlie their actions. But they soon learned that what they might concretely learn from the experience never quite fit any other situation. It was only from an accumulation of such discussions that they learned how to analyze, for themselves, new situations as they arose. Through such analysis they learned to arrive at solutions that were equally constructive to their own growth, to the development of the children, and to their mutual relationships. In short, without engaging in any specific actions, they bettered their way of living with the children.

It would have been easy for me to assemble volumes of such analyses from the records of the Orthogenic School. But those were based on the bizarre actions and thought processes of very disturbed children. Though embodying the same principles, they might not have led so easily to learning experiences on which to base any parallel analysis of what normal parents encounter with their normal children.

Fortunately, for a number of years I conducted group meetings of this kind with the parents (mostly mothers) of normal young children. We all learned so much from these meetings—or so we felt—that after they had gone on for some time we decided to transcribe them electronically. I am very grateful to the participants for their permission to record our discussions. I am thankful to Eugenia Bernoff, who transcribed them, a difficult task which she met with unusual intelligence and devotion. My dear friend and editor, Ruth Marquis, who also attended the meetings, insisted that they contained things of value to all parents and induced me to present them in book form. Together we selected from the volumes of transcriptions a representative sample for publication. In many ways I owe this book to her.

Here too, I should say a few words about how these group meetings came into being. After VE day, and particularly after VJ day, there was a great influx of

17

veterans on all campuses, including the University of Chicago. They were delightful students, since their experiences made what we were trying to teach them more meaningful. They were not only older, but of greater maturity.

Most of the married students lived in several groups of barracks known as the prefabs, and these families quickly developed a rather closely knit social life. Mutual babysitting was only one of many shared activities, such as taking turns at supervising a common playground for toddlers.

While only a limited percentage of all mothers in the prefabs took part in the meetings, they were the mothers most interested in child rearing, and hence the leaders in everything pertaining to children.

The meetings themselves started in a haphazard way. Veterans enrolled in my classes on child development and child psychology showed again and again that what they wanted to learn was not about children in general; repeatedly, during class discussions, they would ask questions about problems they were running into with their own children. Still, a rather large graduate class on child psychology does not always lend itself readily to the discussion of what is concerning a particular father at the moment. One of them might ask me, "Why will Johnny go to the toilet for me, but not for my wife? She wants you to tell me what's wrong with her—that he doesn't go to the toilet for her."

I did not want, in class, to be drawn into discussions of who was right, the father or the mother, in the way he or she handled their child. Still, the concern of these students was real, and it made at least as much sense to me to help them in their difficulties with their children, as to teach them theories about child rearing. At first I tried to solve this impasse by meeting informally with some of the interested fathers among my students.

Even at the very first of these meetings some of the students brought their wives along without asking, and the fourth meeting was attended mainly by mothers, with a sprinkling of fathers. By then it seemed clear that it was the mothers who were most eager to meet with me as a group. Thereafter we met fairly regularly twice a month; our sessions took place in the evening and usually lasted for one and a half hours or a bit longer. The meetings became more and more interesting for all participants, and at one point in 1948, the group being agreeable, we decided to meet in a room that was wired for sound, so that we could transcribe what was said. In this room we continued to meet bimonthly, later every three weeks, and finally once a month; the meetings ended because I could no longer find the time for them, in the spring of 1952.

Most of these mothers were wives of graduate students rather than undergraduates, and, since graduate students often remained at the university for a few years, there was a core of mothers who took part in the meetings pretty regularly throughout their existence. Of course, a few dropped out every year, and a few new parents came to join us. More often than not there were one, two, or three husbands present, but this was about the usual level of participation by fathers.

The number of mothers at any one meeting varied from fifteen or eighteen up to forty. Most of them had small children, although a few had preadolescent children.

Occasionally, also, a grandmother came along—that is, one of the mothers brought along her own mother. Usually the grandmothers were invited in the hope that sitting in on one or two of our meetings might alter some of the preconceived notions. I doubt that this resulted, but, having seen us in operation, they were, I think, more ready to listen to what their daughters told them of what they had learned at the meetings.

Lest the impression be given that these were very sophisticated or highly educated mothers, I should add that, while the majority had some college education, or

19

had finished college, they were by no means a select group. They were intelligent and fairly cultured, but no more so than any average group of young mothers in a good middle-class community. Most of them had married while their husbands were in service.

Many of the conversations will suggest to the reader what a particular home was like and the setting, social and personal, in which events were taking place. The parents' language, rendered as precisely as the transcriptions and readability would permit, should suggest their educational and cultural level and the degree of their real or assumed sophistication.

During the weeks preceding a meeting the mothers thought about, and some of them talked with each other about, what problems they wanted to bring up for discussion; and this influenced to a degree what happened in the meetings. I also thought a bit about the meetings. On the way to each one I usually tried to recall what the trend of the preceding meetings had been, particularly the most recent one: what problems seemed to perturb the group, and how far I thought they had gone in accepting the methods I was trying to teach them. In short, in a rather nondeliberate way I surveyed in my mind what had so far been achieved and what the group seemed ready for as the next step toward greater maturity as parents.

Thus, if there was any planning in my mind, it took the form of deciding what this group needed most to learn, what next steps in learning were suggested by what had happened at the preceding meetings, what loose ends needed tying together, or what the over-all trend of the last several meetings had been.

But, once we began talking, each meeting soon took on a character all its own. After all, though every participant was relating in some fashion to the others—usually in a positive way but many times in a negative fashion—at any one moment the main interaction was nevertheless between a particular mother and me, or between her and one or two other mothers. Thus what was said, and how, and, even more important, how the relationships shaped up at any moment were to a very large degree conditioned by the personalities, worries, attitudes, values, prejudices, and whatnot of a particular subgroup of two, three, or at most four participants.

It is in the nature of such interactions that much of the time the speaker addresses himself mainly to one other person, though he keeps the rest of the group in his mind. He gears what he says first and foremost to this person, basing his reaction on what he knows (or thinks he knows) and feels about him, and on what he hopes this person will derive from what he says or does.

This is no less true in a group, even at times when the speaker is supposedly addressing the whole group. Any teacher knows that he does his best personalized teaching when he focuses his mind on a particular student whom he tries to reach, convince, influence, educate. I say the best "personalized" teaching, because there is also another teaching method—the lecture—which concentrates on the problem being discussed rather than on reaching the audience in a personalized form, as individuals strongly distinct from each other. But these group meetings were not of the lecture type. The main issue for me was to reach the inner feelings and attitudes of the mothers as they pertained to their children, not to make an appeal to their intellectual understanding only, or even primarily. As in any form of teaching, I had to appeal to their rational minds but my purpose was, through the mind, to influence their attitudes.

Thus at any one moment I had to concentrate not so much on teaching them all, though this remained a hoped-for side effect, but on reaching the one mother who had presented a problem or had taken it up where another had left off. In order to achieve this, I had not only to permit but also to encourage the person who spoke up to take the shaping of our mutual relationship into her own hands for the time our interaction lasted. Only then could she become so personally involved that what we talked about might exert some influence on her inner attitudes. For this reason alone, I could not have more than a vaguely preconceived plan about what we ought to do at any one meeting, but had to be guided at any moment by what I perceived to be the nature of the personal relations among me and the group and the mother speaking.

After all, the way in which I handled my relation to them at any one moment, and theirs to me, presented to all of them an image of how any personal relations may be handled. Unless the image of my behavior was in some way in line with the attitude toward their children I was trying to foster in these parents, I would have interfered with the new attitude rather than aided its development. While ours were not parent-child relationships, they were certainly relationships and, as such, had to have something in common with all other personal interactions, including the ones between parent and child. At the least, it had to be true for both that at any moment both partners were shaping the relationship, deciding what should enter into it. This required that neither partner strive for a preconceived goal other than that of making the relationship most fruitful for all who were part of it.

Occasionally I have taken the liberty of adding to the transcripts in order to explain the reasons behind my behavior. But I wish to stress that such reasoning is nearly always hindsight. During an active interchange with some twenty to forty parents there was hardly ever time to reason out what I did. On the other hand, whatever action I took at any time was derived from a great backlog of experience with normal and with very difficult children—both with the children's problems and with those they present to adults trying to help them.

These experiences, and the many occasions I had had to reflect on my own and other adults' behavior in similar situations, suggested to me semi-consciously, almost automatically, how to approach a given problem at the meetings. It also brought vaguely to my mind similar situations I had experienced, and courses of action that had then proved appropriate. Without any deliberate or conscious recall on my part, these past experiences suggested ways of thinking about the problem at hand or what line of reasoning might be especially appropriate to a particular parent and to all others present. Thus how a parent might reason when confronted by a problem, what behavior or action might then be appropriate, was conveyed to the group as much by what I said as by the way I talked or did not talk.

While there was usually no conscious awareness on my part of why exactly I did what I did, nor of my reasons for saying what I said—in short, of my motives and goals during the meetings—there was always the conscious desire to help a particular parent better to understand her child and herself in relation to her child. What happened between us was the result of my bringing my experience, convictions, and attitudes to bear on two particular types of personal relations—the one existing between this parent and her child and the one existing between myself and the group. So, to a large degree what happened was also the unfolding of relationships into which the mother entered as much as I did. Given what I strove for—to have these parents see the true nature of their emotional involvements in their children, and why and how it might be interfering with their being the kind of parents they wanted to be—it was certainly unavoidable, and sometimes desirable, that deep feelings would be aroused in one or another parent. Because these were group meetings, it

23

was impossible for me to gauge correctly or at all times how forceful an anxiety might be evoked by what was talked about, particularly in someone who was listening rather than talking. It is not surprising that some of them had stronger reactions than they could comfortably manage; expecting this, I moved quite cautiously in the first few meetings. But the majority of the mothers who attended regularly were willing to explore their deeper feelings, since they wanted to learn more about what was behind their attitudes to their children.

In my own work with the parents of very disturbed children I knew that they were themselves often emotionally disturbed, if for no other reason than their deep anxiety about their children's difficulties and their long involvement in the child's problems. I had expected parallel strong resistance to gaining insight in this group. Much to my surprise, I found that these normal parents of normal children showed little such resistance and none or very few of the neurotic defenses I had expected. With this realization, and following the lead of the majority, I moved rather rapidly and directly into discussing topics and attitudes that under other circumstances, and with emotionally disturbed parents, might have been fraught with emotional danger.

Both by proceeding in this way, and by what we discussed and how we discussed it, the meetings proved too upsetting to a very few parents, both fathers and mothers. They either froze up, or totally misunderstood what we were talking about, became angry, or in other ways showed that what happened was too distressing to them. Their number was very small: I did not keep an exact count, but in retrospect I feel certain that it amounted to less than the 5 per cent of deviant cases one must expect in any random selection. Usually such parents dropped out after the meeting that proved too disturbing to them; at the most, they came once again before dropping out permanently. Thus they spontaneously removed themselves from an experience that was not useful to them.

At the other extreme, for a very few parents what we discussed was too elementary to hold their attention—or so they claimed. They wanted to press at all times, and immediately, for what they considered "deep interpretations." The difficulty was that they also tried to tell the questioning parent what was wrong with her, or her child.

Since my interest lay not in telling, but in helping to find out—not in teaching what was wrong, but in conveying a method of investigation—I had to interfere with these participants. It then developed that learning about processes seemed of less interest to them than making known their wider knowledge. Since they violated what I tried to establish as a prime principle—namely, that no person can know what is disturbing another person, that the best he can achieve is to help another person himself to discover what troubles him—I was quite insistent with them, and they soon dropped out as well. The two or three parents in this category also remained for no more than two sessions.

While none of this was ever spelled out, the group soon understood that the great profit to them was not in particular knowledge—which could, at best, apply to only special situations—but in a method and process of finding out that could serve them in all situations.

For example, they learned that I was not there to say at what age a child should begin sharing his toys. What I could help them to see was that a child never does what he does "just for attention." Always behind it lie at least two problems: why he needs attention at the moment, and why he chose this behavior of all possible ways of reaching his goal. To dismiss what the child does as simply an attention-getting device means only one thing to him: we do not take him seriously enough to find out why he wants what he wants. He also takes it to mean that our evaluation of

25

his motives is more important to us than what his motives really are. Most of all, it teaches him that we do not think of what he does as being serious or purposeful. And since his parents, who are so important to him, think that he acts without plan or purpose, he concludes he must be "pretty dumb."

Parents had to come to realize how all of us are apt to ignore a child, or to respond with annoyance, when he wants something from us, as against the response to behavior that is not directed toward us, when he is simply pursuing his own business, though we dislike how he goes about it. This led to the realization of how apt we are to dislike the child's interfering with our business, but how ready we are to interfere with his—and how this convinces him that we think whatever we do is important, and whatever he does is not.

Parents learned, too, that there was little profit in asking what was the best way to stop a child from biting other children unless they could tell me why he was biting in the first place. That spanking *versus* not spanking was beside the point, while ignoring the problem solved nothing. Even letting the child "express" his anger was risky business—as I have already related—since we cannot let children go around biting.

Instead, what was often a useful approach was to ask oneself: "If I were a child, why would I do this?" or "What could make *me* want to bite another person?" It then became apparent that biting wasn't really the issue, but merely the symptom, just as spanking is not an issue but simply a consequence (perhaps of biting). The problem of discipline usually melted away under questioning, just as fever disappears when the underlying disease is correctly identified and given appropriate treatment. But by learning how to discover, and then to alleviate, the pressures that might lead a child to bite (or the parents to wish to spank), such questions as being permissive or restrictive even ceased to arise.

This was nicely summarized by one of the mothers

toward the end of the first year. At the beginning of our sessions (she told me), when the mothers discussed their children and their problems with each other, they would review courses of action I had suggested in the past in what seemed like a parallel situation. But toward the end of the year they no longer asked each other what they thought I would consider the "right" answer but, instead, speculated about how I would probably go about trying to discover what was wrong.

I did not select the particular discussions presented here because they were exceptionally startling, or made a theoretical point, or because they were in any other fashion important. As a matter of fact, the range of problems showed an unending variety, and even a book ten times as large as this one could not begin to cover them all.

Typically, I did not include a discussion of masturbation, because such loaded issues tend to obscure the fact that what I was trying to achieve was a method of analysis, not a series of recommendations. If the relation between parent and child is basically a good one, then the way that masturbation is handled is not likely to make too much difference. Even when a parent has "learned" that masturbation is permissible, if the child is otherwise frustrated in his personal relations with his parents, he may resort to excessive and isolating self-stimulation, with as much potential damage as if the parent had denied him the freedom to masturbate.

Thus what I tried to include here were the most everyday examples I could find, and I hope they will be read as such—small events that are likely to happen in any child's day and that need to be handled as they occur. If parents respond to such events unthinkingly, they influence the child in one way; handled sensitively, they have an entirely different impact on the child. In any case, these—the many small experiences that form the essence of our lives—are, added up, what form the child's personality and the relations between him and ourselves.

Depending on how we handle such daily interactions, then, our children's personality development and their relationship to life will take one of several courses. No single event need have especially great impact, but it is amazing how such little experiences make up, in the long run, a good life or a pretty miserable one. And all this occurs without anything really terribly important having happened, good or bad.

I

Why Would I Do This?

I'm Somebody Else

DR.B.: Well, Christmas is over. It's a big time in your child's life and in yours too, but not always an easy one. I trust you've all weathered it successfully. Yes? [*Nodding to a mother*] Go ahead.

MOTHER: I have a question, Dr. Bettelheim. My little girl is two and a half and I have another girl three months old. During the summer my older girl began to pretend she was different animals. One day she would be a mouse and would go around squeaking all day. Then after the baby came she wasn't anything for a while. But about six weeks ago she took on the identity of the little girl next door. It started out that she was Kathy—that's the little girl's name. I was Kathy's mother, and our baby was supposed to be Brian—that's the name of the little girl's baby brother. And she insists very firmly that we have to call her Kathy, and our baby has to be referred to as a boy, and be called Brian. Now all this time I've just been playing along with her and calling her by those names. But I'm just wondering how long it's going to go on.

DR. B.: For as long as you go along with it. And if it were just a question of humoring her, there wouldn't be anything wrong with it. But while many children, when they're a little past two, say they don't like their names, if she can play for a whole day at being an animal, she's intelligent enough and can express herself well enough to be able to tell you why she wants to be called by a different name. Have you asked her that?

MOTHER: No, I haven't. I don't know if she understands, or how much of it, when you ask, "Why?" She herself has just started asking about "Why."

DR. B.: Now look. To convey to you that she wants to be called Kathy and that she wants her baby sister to be called by a certain name calls for quite a vocabulary. This vocabulary she couldn't have acquired and used intelligently without understanding the "Why" of it.

MOTHER: No. What I mean is, sometimes I've asked her "Why" about other things, and she doesn't seem to understand.[1]

DR. B: That's strange . . .

MOTHER: Well . . . but I was just wondering about her insisting on the baby being a boy.

DR. B.: Okay, let's look for a moment at what we can do if we don't understand what a child is up to. This is of general interest. If a child does something that doesn't make sense, or that we don't understand, but that we want to understand, what's always a good way of finding out? One possibility is to play along with the notion of the child and see where it leads us. That's what this mother is doing, but it's gotten her nowhere. What else can we do?

SECOND MOTHER: Well, she started out by wanting to be called by the name of a friend of hers.

DR. B.: That's going over the facts we already know; that's not finding out the cause.

1. A frequent and understandable error of parents. They ask their young child to explain things he does without plan or inner motive. The young child does not know what is meant, or how *he* can explain what to him is self-evident or in no need of thought or explanation. But the same child, when beset by deep needs to which he has found a solution (in this case, by changing identity), can well explain the situation because here he is deeply involved. Just because a young child cannot explain to us, or even understand our question, when *we* are curious and involved but he is not, we must not therefore assume that he cannot do so when he *is* deeply curious and involved.

SECOND MOTHER: Well, she could talk to her.

DR. B.: Sure, but the mother's already done that. What else can you do if you don't understand strange behavior in your child?

THIRD MOTHER: Go and ask somebody. That's why we come to you!

DR. B.: Yes, but I'm not always so conveniently around.

FOURTH MOTHER: I'd ask myself, when would I act this way.

DR. B.: Exactly! But why do you say it so hesitantly? So often when you give the wrong answer you're very forceful, but with the right answer you're hesitant. We just don't trust ourselves enough to believe we have the answers right in us, if we just dared to look into ourselves. But that's where we have to look for all the difficult answers. All right, so the first thing I ask myself when there's strange behavior I don't understand is: "When would I do this; and if I do so, why would I do it?"

MOTHER: Well, my first thought was that she didn't want to be herself any more.

DR.B.: Exactly! So what *did* you do? What did you show her through your behavior?

MOTHER: Well, I asked somebody else.

DR.B.: That's a possibility. Let's have an experiment and ask someone else right now. We have many good-looking men and women here tonight. What if I wanted to be as good-looking as they are? What would I do? Would I change my name to one of theirs?

FOURTH MOTHER: No, you should be encouraged to be yourself.

DR. B.: Exactly! It's not a question of who I want to be, or what you'd like to be. There's no way out, my girl . . . there's no way out; we just have got to be what we are!

MOTHER: You mean, I should just let her suffer it out?

DR. B.: That's right! She's stuck with herself, with her own name, with the baby sister! And so are you. Well, let's not call it "stuck," though she may feel it that way. We can give it a much pleasanter name. What I'm driving at is that you're the mother and should know better. Yet by entering this play, you not only enforce her idea that she can be somebody else, that she can change the sex of her brothers or sisters, that she can pretend she has different parents, but that you agree that all this would be nice. Do you think that's right?

MOTHER: Well, this is what I did. You know her real name is Pat, and the baby is Karen. So when I'd talk to her I would talk to her as Pat and the baby as Karen, and she'd keep correcting me—that she was Kathy and the baby was Brian, and she would get real mad about it.

DR. B.: Of course! Who wouldn't like to change at will? If I thought I could change at will and somebody interfered with me, I'd get mad, too!"

MOTHER: Yes, but the other thing I thought about was—at this two-and-a-half-year-old stage, when they're so domineering, I thought they should be humored as much as they can. So I was torn between the two things!

DR. B.: The two-and-a-half-year-old is supposed to be humored?

MOTHER: Well . . . that's what I read.

DR.B.: And you don't want to be humored?

MOTHER: Sure, everybody wants to be humored!

DR. B.: All right! Then why talk about the two-and-a-half-year-old as somebody who wants to be humored?

MOTHER: Oh, I don't mean it particularly, but I thought that was an age . . .

DR. B.: But it's true for all ages . . . that we want to be humored. The question is: how do we want to be humored? And does it do us any good to be humored in this particular way? Do you really think—if you dreamed of being the most beautiful woman in the world—do you really think it would be of service to you if everybody humored you in that idea?

MOTHER: No, of course not.

DR. B.: Then why should it be any different for your two-and-a-half-year-old? So the real problem is: When should you humor her and when not. And how can you humor her? How do we all want to be humored? But let's drop these generalities and get back to your little girl. Why do you think she started the game?

MOTHER: Because she wanted attention.

DR. B.: So do we all. But you and I still wouldn't know what she wanted. Let's not go through that again. It's a fascinating topic, but . . .

SECOND MOTHER: Because of the new baby, I think.

DR. B.: Maybe, but we shouldn't shove everything off on the new baby. It's a first guess, and a very reasonable one, but I've seen it misfire. Mommy's suddenly interested in something else. It needn't be the new baby, but the new baby is a wonderful excuse.

MOTHER: You mean it could have been something else? But it happened at about the time the baby was six weeks old.

DR. B.: But she started with the animals before that.

MOTHER: Oh . . . yes. The animals were before the baby came.

DR. B.: Yes. So why should we assume it was the baby? It started when you were pregnant, and maybe there was less time to play with her. In any case, we've made progress. We no longer say that the child just wants to be humored, which would be pushing it all on the poor child. Let's say instead that something is suddenly missing in life, and that the child, in her own childish way, is trying to make up for the deficiency. You see, I'm not worried about your child. What she did was quite reasonable in terms of the means a two-and-a-half-year-old can muster for coping with a difficult situation. What worries me is that you fell for it instead of presenting her with a reasonable way out.

You could have told her, "You can pretend to be a mouse if you like, or a lion, or to be Kathy for a little while. But it's a pretend game, because you can't be Kathy, and particularly, you cannot change the sex of the baby." Because that's one of the greatest fears of young children anyway—that sex can be changed at will. So by humoring her, by joining her so seriously, you may have increased her anxiety instead of concentrating on making it less desirable for her to be Kathy.

Now, how you do that is another story. That we have to investigate in terms of what you can do for your child at the moment, and that may be harder. But at the least you have to insist on your and her and the baby's true name and sex, on who her real parents are, and so forth.

MOTHER: She's even insisted I was Kathys' mommy.

DR. B.: Sure. Because if you're Kathy's mommy, pretty soon she's Kathy herself. Do you feel that this answers your question?

MOTHER: Well, I'm wondering. Do you think I should just do it real suddenly? Tomorrow, when she starts to pretend again . . .

DR. B.: Yes, I think you should stop right away. That doesn't mean you should forcefully forbid her her fantasies. But you can quietly tell her who you are and who she is. On the other hand, you have no right to stop her game unless you have some plan about how you're going to close the gap she was trying to fill by this living in a make-believe world. To take away the game without filling the need for it is just no good. It'll only force her to invent something different and maybe more devious.

MOTHER: What do you mean? Showing her why she did it?

DR. B.: No, that you cannot do. All you can do is to continue your explanation till she gets her fill of it, but without getting angry or upset. Say that she is she, you are you, and the baby is Karen. She'll get so bored by it she'll invent another game, but a more realistic one. On the other hand, I think you should play with her a good deal, spend a lot of time with her, and maybe your husband could help—so that the wish to be somebody else will subside because she'll enjoy being herself so much more.

MOTHER: Well, we do try. We spend lots of time with her . . .

DR. B.: That's fine. You do that, and let's see what happens.

[One month later]

MOTHER: I want to tell you about the results of some suggestions you offered. Remember when I told you about my little girl who adopted another name, and one for the baby too?

DR. B.: Oh, yes, I wanted to hear about what happened.

MOTHER: Well, the next morning we started out by calling her Pat, and she said "No," she was Kathy. So we told her, "No," she was Pat. This happened several times, and then it was dropped. We just continued to call her Pat and she didn't say anything. Then a little later in the morning I said something about Karen, the baby, and she said, "No, the baby is Brian." So I said, "No, she's Karen."

DR. B.: Good for you!

MOTHER: Well, and you also said I should ask her "Why," and at the time I didn't think she would understand and she didn't. I said, "Why do you think Karen is Brian?" and she said, "Because he's a boy!" and I said, "Well, why do you think she's a boy?" and she said, "Because he's a boy," and that was her only answer.[2] So I said, "Well, no, honey, you know she's a

2. In view of my comment in note 1, I might add here that this is exactly the type of explanation one might hope for in such a young child. She tells us that she wanted the names

girl, and her name is Karen," and we went over that several times and then she dropped it and everything was fine after that. I also announced to my husband when I came home that there wasn't going to be any more cooking or baking or cleaning; that I was just going to spend my days with the children for a while. Well, I didn't go so far as to have sandwiches at every meal, but as far as dinner went, we just had what was very simple and I would just wait till he got home to fix it.

DR. B.: And he hasn't lost any appreciable weight?

MOTHER: Oh, no! And after that, everything was fine as far as the names were concerned. Yesterday, at two different times when she was unhappy about something, and I called her Pat, she tried to tell me she was Kathy. So I just told her again she was Pat.

DR. B.: So you see now that it was all a reaction to being unhappy.

MOTHER: Very definitely! And anyhow, since then her behavior's improved very much. She's much happier, and she hasn't at all gone back to the other names. In fact, it got to the point where I couldn't even call her my little pumpkin because she'd say, "No, I'm Pat!"

DR. B.: That'll teach you!

MOTHER: Anyhow, it's been working out very well!

DR. B.: Well, that's very gratifying. But don't fool yourself; if you hadn't spent more time with your child, just insisting on the names wouldn't have done it. The one without the other wouldn't have worked.

MOTHER: Oh, yes. I know it. But I'd fallen into this

changed because she did not want a baby sister, but would have liked having a baby brother. He, being of the other sex, would have threatened her identity less, including her identity as a girl, or so it may have seemed to her. Thus unbeknownst to the mother, her answer, "Because he's a boy," irrational as it sounds on an intellectual level, is a correct answer in terms of her emotional needs.

pattern of not spending much time with her, and I hadn't realized it until you spoke about it. Then I could see very clearly what I'd been doing. Oh, yes ... and the other thing she's started, since all this happened, is that she's suddenly started going to the toilet and having her B.M.s in the toilet.

DR.B.: Well, since we've achieved such a miracle cure ...

MOTHER: No, really. It's not a miracle. It's just what should be.

DR. B.: Well, believe me, to do what we should do in bringing children up in this world of ours sometimes seems little short of a miracle!

2

The Potty and the Piggy Bank

DR. B.: Let's get started. Who wants to begin?

MOTHER: I do. I have a problem that started up a few weeks before Christmas. My little girl will be three in a couple of months and up to recently we've never made an issue of whether she was wet or dry. If she made a mistake we simply changed her clothes and tried to point out that there were advantages to staying dry, and we'd prefer it if she did. But just before Christmas, and all during the holidays, she was very close to three of the grandparents, and they thought it was just terrible that she got wet all the time, at her advanced age. It got pretty bad and now she's wetter than ever. But I sort of got into the pattern too because they made me so nervous, and I've been feeling pretty guilty about it. She keeps getting wet, and I've started to wash more and more, and I just think we're off on the wrong track.

DR. B.: Okay. Any suggestions? You've all heard the problem. Where do we begin?

SECOND MOTHER: She could send the diapers out.

DR. B.: Why?

SECOND MOTHER: So the child doesn't wet them just so her mother will have to wash them, like a sort of revenge.

THIRD MOTHER: Well, I don't see why. It wasn't the

mother, it was the grandparents who made an issue of it.

MOTHER: No, it was my fault too, because the influence of my parents and the family made me a little bit touchy about it. Now I can't stop it, because every time I see them on week-ends, they say, "Well, how's she doing? Have you made any progress?" By now my only idea is perhaps to show her we don't care; to try to get over being upset about it. But I don't know exactly how to do that.

DR. B.: Let's have some more suggestions. Lots of you must find yourselves in the same boat.

SECOND MOTHER: What about asking her?

MOTHER: We do ask her, and she says, "No," she doesn't want to go.

DR. B.: She wants to wet?

MOTHER: No, she says she doesn't want to wet. She says, "I'm going to stay dry," but then she doesn't.

DR. B.: Never? She never goes to the toilet?

MOTHER: M-m-m . . . every once in a while. Maybe once every day.

DR. B.: When? What are the times when she does go?

MOTHER: There doesn't seem to be a particular time. But I know one thing—in nursery school, where she goes every morning, she's never once been wet. They toilet the children once, in the middle of the morning.

DR. B.: What potty arrangements do you have at home?

MOTHER: We have a little step stool leading to the toilet, and one of these round seats that doesn't have a gap in it, so she can sit comfortably without falling in.

DR. B.: Okay. But why can she do it at nursery school and not at home? Have you asked her?

MOTHER: I've asked myself and—

DR. B.: No, no. Don't ask yourself until you've first tried to find out from her. Have you asked *her?*

MOTHER: No, I haven't.

DR. B.: Why not?

MOTHER: Maybe I underestimate her intelligence. I've asked her why she preferred to stay wet and not go to the potty.

DR. B.: But obviously she *doesn't* prefer to stay wet. She prefers it only at home.

MOTHER: Well, I'll have to try that one.

DR. B.: Because I really think that if something hasn't gone wrong, a three-year-old should be well able, if she wishes, to go to the toilet. And if she can do it at nursery school she can certainly do it at home. Therefore, we must ask ourselves: why not at home and why at nursery school? Well, we've heard now about the grandparents, and the excitement, and the nervousness and all that. But we haven't really asked: when did it break down? When exactly did the change occur?

MOTHER: Oh, about the time one of the grandparents came and stayed with us for a while.

DR. B.: Right away?

MOTHER: No, but in a couple of days.

SECOND MOTHER: Pardon me, but do you think it might have anything to do with your going out to sell brushes?

MOTHER: No, because I've done that over a year and we'd been going along very smoothly. It was just assumed she would do it when she was good and ready, and she was doing fine. This abrupt change came almost simultaneously with the arrival of the devoted grandmother.

DR. B.: Of course, blaming the grandparents is a convenient way out. But at least we've had one constructive suggestion: don't wash her things yourself, and don't rush. "So you're wet! So you wet yourself. What do you come running to me for? Why do you complain to me?"

MOTHER: Okay. I've got two kittens and their puddles. I don't think I'll be bothered by hers.

DR. B.: Ah, now we have kittens! When did you get the kittens?

MOTHER: Oh, long ago, way before the grandmother arrived.

DR. B.: It's got to be the grandparents! By golly, we're going to look around until we can blame it on them!

MOTHER: I think the kittens arrived about three months ago.

DR. B.: Yes? And why did they arrive? What do they do for the family?

MOTHER: Oh, they're an eternal amusement. The two of them play together, and they play with us and with her. They seem quite a welcome addition.

DR. B.: And what sex are they?

MOTHER: They're both ex-males.

DR. B.: Does the child know that?

MOTHER: No-o.

DR. B.: How do you know?

MOTHER: Well, she's never inquired.

DR. B.: That's a good reason!

MOTHER: Well, I don't think she has the anatomical information to find out by examination.

DR. B.: I wouldn't be too sure.

SECOND MOTHER: Wouldn't she be curious even if she didn't look?

DR. B.: I don't know. But I'm very much against castrated animals in the house.

MOTHER: Really? Why?

DR. B.: [turning] Anybody here know why? Yes?

SECOND MOTHER: The children are afraid someone will do that to them.

DR. B.: That's right. Where did you learn that?

SECOND MOTHER: Well, you told us.

DR. B.: Oh, you learned it here?

[*Burst of laughter*]

MOTHER: Come on. Let's get on with this cat business. That's something I never imagined would influence her. How would she know about it? From hearing it discussed?

DR. B.: I don't know. That's certainly a possibility, but I wouldn't know. As a matter of fact I'm not at all sure there is such a connection in her mind at this point. But I do know that sooner or later the castration will make trouble, if it hasn't already.

MOTHER: Oh? I can't see how.

DR. B.: I don't know how. But three years is an age, and particularly on entering nursery school, when the normal child becomes most aware of the sex differences. As you know, nursery school toilets aren't usually private, and then the children observe one another. If there are children at home who are very close in age, and of different sexes, it can start earlier. But particularly for the only child, or if you have two children of the same sex, and the parents haven't been too immodest in front of their children, that's usually the age, in our culture, when children become keenly aware of the sex differences.

Any nursery school teacher can tell you that much of the time during the first days is spent in the toilet watching others. Usually it's the child with very deep repressions who doesn't do that. As a matter of fact, if you ask a small child what they do in nursery school, he often says, "We go and get undressed and go to the toilet. Then we have a rest and then we go to the toilet, and then we get dressed and go home again."

Now that's a fairly adequate description of the time schedule, but only fairly adequate. Because they play and do other things too. But if the child is free to convey what is really of fascination to him, it's exactly that. They're interested in going to the toilet, the resting, the going to the toilet, maybe having a snack, and then getting dressed and going home. Is that what you've observed with your own children who go to the nursery? [*Sounds of assent and amusement*] Isn't that what they say? And then some parents jump to the conclusion that nursery school teachers don't know how to play or what to do with children!

In rare cases it might be a true summary of nursery school; it is in all cases a summary of what is meaningful to newcomers. Now, once they've started to look for sex differences, they're going to look for them everywhere. And if your child hasn't started yet, she will start very soon. But then, to have males that are not males is not a good idea. You will readily understand that if your child sees a three-legged dog, where one leg was run over by a car or something. The kid will be scared. Well, isn't that a part of the body, too, what these kittens are missing?

MOTHER: I'm thunderstruck. I never thought about it.

DR. B.: And the next step will be, "How come these kittens have something missing? Who did it to them? Who arranged for it?" Well . . . who did?

MOTHER: We did.

DR. B.: Yet you know how strongly children identify with little animals? How they feel much closer to them than to adult human beings? That's another reason they may think that what happens to animals might happen to them.

SECOND MOTHER: Remember what you told me once, about your little girl putting the cat on the toilet, just as if it were a child?

DR. B.: Did it work?

MOTHER: No! It fell in! I had to pull it out!

[*Outburst of laughter*]

DR. B.: Well! There we have the traumatic experience of going to the toilet: "The kitten fell in, and

45

maybe I'll fall in, too! At nursery school no kittens fall in, so in nursery school the toilet is safe."

SECOND MOTHER: Didn't that happen about the time your girl started wetting again?

MOTHER: For heaven's sake! It did!

SECOND MOTHER: And wasn't that when the grandmother came?

MOTHER: Oh my gosh, that's right!

DR. B.: I told you not to try too hard with the grandmas.

MOTHER: Well! Just because you may be real smart!

DR. B.: No, your kid is smart. She can connect things, and draw conclusions.

MOTHER: I'll be jiggered! Well, then you suggest getting rid of the cats?

DR. B.: No, not necessarily.

MOTHER: Does anybody want a life-sized cat?

SECOND MOTHER: Why not try the potty in the kitchen, too?

DR. B.: She can try it if she wants to, but I don't think it will get to the center of the problem.

SECOND MOTHER: But shouldn't she go back to the little potty chair? Don't children feel safer on those?

DR. B.: Some children do. But look. One of the ways to encourage them to do it the way we do is to show them they're coming closer and closer to grown-up human beings. But to make use of this mechanism you have to get them to do it in a way as close to what you do as possible. But let's be realistic, too. Probably what happened was a combination of many circumstances.

The cat fell in, and that may have started it all. But that wasn't the only thing! It may have been the cat falling in, it may have been the castration of the cats, or your feelings about the grandmother and her disapproval; maybe it was this and maybe it was that. I don't know. Here we can just hunt around, and help you uncover the facts. The rest is up to you. I'm sure this discussion has suggested several courses of action to you. Try out one after another till something works, and let's talk about it again in two weeks or a month.

[*Two weeks later*]

SECOND MOTHER: Tell us ... what happened with your cats?

MOTHER: Well, I don't want to give the cats away, and I've decided not to. But the other problem, about the wetting, that's solved. I'll explain about the cats, though. I've been raised with castrated cats and I don't, to my knowledge, have any queer complexes.

DR. B.: Oh, that we know!

MOTHER: Well, it's very easy to notice if a dog has lost its accessories, but it's very difficult to find out whether or not a cat is a male, a female, or an ex-male. So we're keeping the cats. They're fine. But the business of the wetting was really driving us crazy, and it reached a high point when—

DR. B.: Isn't it strange, only the human misbehavior drives us crazy, not the cats'. Which just goes to show that what drives us crazy has little to do with reality, but a great deal to do with our expectations. Of cats we don't expect socialized behavior, so they don't drive us crazy. Of our children we do, so they drive us crazy. Maybe if we expected less of our children and trusted that with a little teaching they'd eventually learn it just as cats do, they'd stop driving us crazy and would learn it as easily as any well-trained cat.

But don't mind my suggestion that we use as much forebearance with our children as we do with our pets. Go on.

MOTHER: Well, when I last talked to you, Judy was wet many, many times during the day.

DR. B.: So you went to talk to Dr. Bettelheim about it.

MOTHER: So we went to talk to Dr. Bettelheim, and I came home and told Jim all about it, and he scratched

47

his head and said, "Well, what'll we do?" But in the meantime, we had an opportunity to go to another psychologist and listen to what he had to say.

DR. B.: A real one!

MOTHER: Well, no-o. But anyway, we came home from that meeting with the idea that we weren't supposed to be even bothered about it. We're convinced that his attitude is correct, just as yours is. If you could absolutely divorce yourself of any feeling against wetting, the child will eventually assume the responsibility by himself.

DR. B.: Very sensible advice . . . if you can do it.

MOTHER: Well, for the next two days, Jim and I were steadily divorcing ourselves from being upset, and when Judy wet her pants, we'd tell her, "Oh, that's all right; we don't mind." But she knew very well we were still fuming underneath. So it got pretty bad one day. I was just washing pants right and left. I still don't want to send it out to the laundry because it costs so much . . . Anyway, Jim started to tear his hair and say, "Oh, the hell with the psychologist. Let's do what we feel is right." So I said, "What do we feel is right?" [*Much laughter at this point*] So he said, "Well, let's tell her we don't like it. Let's be honest and tell her we don't like it, that we're tired of the whole thing and won't she please cooperate."

DR. B.: How old is she, again?

MOTHER: She'll be three next month. That's a pretty ripe old age for wetting pants all day.

DR. B.: No, but go ahead.

MOTHER: Well, we thought it was. So, we weren't going to punish her for it. That's something we've learned from psychologists and it's sunk in. But every time she wet her pants we told her we didn't like it, that we'd much prefer it if she took care of those things on the potty. We got down the old potty seat, dug it out and repaired it, and she was happy and would sit on it, though she still made mistakes. But then she dug out, from an old corner where we'd hidden it, a great big piggy bank.

Now, she doesn't know what a bank is and we've never told her. She has no idea that money means anything. But she discovered that buttons, and metal discs of any kind, safety pins, pennies, all go into that slot, disappear, and rattle around, and it's fun to put them in. So we left it out within easy reach and we told Judy that every time she managed to go to the potty before she got her panties wet, we would give her something nice to put into the slot. So I got a whole batch of pennies . . .

DR. B.: Yes, but the psychologist doesn't like that at all!

MOTHER: But it worked!

DR. B.: Spanking works too! If you want to make your child scared or obstinate, or what is described in books as an anal erotic, go ahead and do that.

MOTHER: Well, there's another sequel. We didn't press it. We didn't remind her every time she did it that she was going to get a penny, or something. And in the last three days it's almost gone from the picture.

DR. B.: Yes, but it isn't gone from her mind.

MOTHER: But she's still going to the potty and doing good.

DR. B.: With the same reasoning you can convince me that a good spanking does the child and the mother a lot of good. I've never doubted it. But I just don't like it.

MOTHER: Well, actually, I think . . .

DR. B.: It's the expedient way, it's not sound psychology. I'm sorry I cannot agree with you. You're welcome to experiment with your child as you like. I have no objection to your telling your child you don't like it. I have no objection to your telling your child, "I wish you would go to the potty. I just cannot stand your wetting." I don't think it's the best way, but at least it's an honest way.

MOTHER: Well, I think that's what cleared up the atmosphere.

DR. B.: That I'm ready to believe.

MOTHER: Anyway, she's wet maybe once or twice during the day and we've never done anything about it.

DR. B.: Look, a good spanking after each wetting might have achieved it even sooner. But what you do is a more subtle torture. We don't stretch prisoners on the rack any more. We've refined our methods. We don't spank children any more, but we do things that are psychologically just as unsound and upset their lives just as effectively.

MOTHER: But she can still put in pennies whenever she wants to. It doesn't have to be tied up with that.

DR. B.: *You* have tied it up! If she had invented it on her own, I would have been skeptical, but I wouldn't be outraged. But you, as a mother, should be more intelligent. If that child out of her own emotional needs had found a way out such as you describe with the piggy bank—it ain't good, but all right, we can handle it. But you have established a connection between money and elimination which never existed before in her mind. And money is something very important in our society, don't fool yourself. I wish I had more. You have established a wrong connection between two such terribly important things in our society: money and cleanliness. You, the mother, have established that. You, who are the world for your child.

MOTHER: I wish ... that's ... it does sound terribly wrong. I wish I could start over again.

DR. B.: But I wish you would ask first, and then do. That's what these meetings are for. Well, our time is up. But we'll be meeting again ... So let's just say, "live and learn."

In this rather heated incident, the speaking mother showed strong negative involvement with her daughter's wetting. Hindsight now suggests that my efforts to make her aware of this collapsed early in the discussion when she was not startled to realize that her child could use the toilet at nursery school but not at home. Had she been able to fully grasp what this meant, she could also have seen the difference: that at nursery school there were no clashes between her own wishes and the child's opposite desires.

I think I was also in error when I let myself get sidetracked by the castrated cats. Though a useful digression because it brought to light the fact that the little girl saw one of the kittens fall into the toilet, it probably was not central to the problem.

As the discussion of two weeks later reveals, the basic issue was the mother's strong feelings about her child's wetting. I recognized this in a fashion when I told her that the advice of the psychologist she had consulted was correct, but that the issue was not the soundness of his advice but whether it could be followed by anyone who felt as strongly as she did about the problem. The parents were unable, in fact, to do so, as suggested by the statement, "Oh, the hell with the psychologist!"

Very early in this discussion my direct question, "She *wants* to wet?" was meant to suggest that the mother did not take her child's statements seriously. Or to put it differently, the mother could see only her own logic, but did not try to understand the logic of her child. When the child told her mother that she didn't want to go to the toilet, but also said she didn't want to wet herself, the mother saw it as a contradiction, not a conflict. She could not see that it is quite possible for a child to want to be dry but not to want to eliminate in the toilet. My question was designed to show her that the two desires are by no means incompatible.

When as adults we find ourselves in similar situations, we can readily accept that such conflicts

51

happen to us. The desire to save money may be quite strong, but the temptation or desire to spend it may turn out to be stronger. Hence, despite the continuation of a strong desire (to save), an even stronger desire (to spend) may win out. The parent sees no illogic in his own behavior; but he sees it in that of his child simply because old conflicting desires about elimination no longer exist in himself.

Here, as in so many cases, it was my purpose to convince the mother that the first step in understanding children's behavior is to accept that a child has as good reasons for his behavior as the parent has for his; that if the child's statements seem contradictory (she wants to be dry, but she does not want to go to the toilet) the contradiction may be due to lack of understanding on the part of the adult. Once this is accepted, most parents will try to understand the child's behavior instead of dismissing it as illogical. But once they do try, they usually end up understanding it and are therefore better able to find a solution acceptable to parent and child.

I might also have taken up earlier the mother's notion that she had stopped punishing her child— as if being critical each time the child wet herself did not constitute punishment.

Perhaps most of all, this discussion was included because it demonstrates that merely finding out what causes a child's behavior solves nothing unless the understanding leads to a change in parental attitude. An understanding *was* gained of the likely motives behind the child's behavior; but neither parent was willing to change his attitude toward the child's wetting, despite their greater understanding. Still, the discussion led to some concessions—chiefly, that the stricter punishment and recrimination were replaced by milder criticism.

Also the parents no longer insisted on the child's going on the big toilet, once they realized that their toilet might be scary. Instead, they took the positive action of repairing and reintroducing the potty seat and of encouraging the child to use it. But this was not enough. They were unable to realize that their critical attitude was what created the problem in the first place, for if toilets per se had been scary, the child could not have used them at nursery school.

This leads us to a further lesson to be learned from the incident—namely, how a compulsive symptom comes into being. It also demonstrates the readiness of children to meet their parents more than half way. Since the parents lowered their strictures by being milder in their criticism and by dropping other punishments, and since they took the positive step of reinstating the potty, the child on her own took even greater steps to meet parental demands.

Unfortunately, those demands were based on a critical attitude rather than on a delight, for example, over the child's ingenuity in protecting herself against danger (if cats fall into the toilet, so may I). Therefore, what resulted was not true growth but only a stunted adjustment to parental demands—that is, not the realistic solution of an impasse, but an attempt to circumvent it through a neurotic symptom.

The symptom chosen by the girl expresses both of her wishes: that she should not be forced to give up something permanently but be allowed to hold on to it, and that she obey the parental wish to eliminate body content into the toilet. So, when forced to let go of body content into the toilet, she held on to money instead, by putting something into the piggy bank when eliminating. This is one of the few examples provided by the meetings which made it clear how a child spontaneously developed a compulsive symptom in response to arbitrary pressures; where she wished to conform but could not readily do so. For this reason the discussion was included in the book.

3

Flesh and Blood

MOTHER: My problem is with my little boy, who'll be four in April. Recently he's become very anxious about ... well, what it amounts to is, where does the meat come from? It actually came to a head on Thanksgiving, but I realize now it's been coming on for some time. I suppose he got it from nursery school, because I've never mentioned it.

DR. B.: Yes, it's a great socializing experience.

MOTHER: Anyway, he would ask me, "I suppose we're going to have turkey for Thanksgiving?" and I'd say "Yes" without thinking about it. But he'd ask me this about once a day. Then on Thanksgiving he asked, "Where's the turkey?" So I opened the oven and said, "There's the turkey," and there was just a shocked expression on his face. Then I realized that of course he was expecting a live turkey. So he wouldn't touch it. He wouldn't touch it at all. He wouldn't eat it.

DR. B.: Maybe he was looking forward to playing with this turkey?

MOTHER: And I didn't know what to say.

DR. B.: That's quite an embarrassing experience.

MOTHER: It is! But that isn't all. Now, whenever any meat appears on the table or we have fish, he wants to know where its head is. What's happened to it? And he keeps saying he doesn't like it, that the fishes don't like this. But it really worries him. He seems quite anxious and keeps complaining about it. Then one day he said to me, "Do you remember that time you were cooking the chicken and it was lying right on the pan?" I tried to explain to him that when you're cooking a chicken it isn't just lying on the pan; that it doesn't feel anything. But I didn't want to get started. I don't want to tell him it was killed.

DR. B.: Well, what else? You can't give him the impression that he's going to be eating a live chicken.

MOTHER: Well . . . what am I going to say? Because that's really what's bothering him. I wish I'd never started with nursery school. He's at the stage now where he's terrified of animals in any form. And at nursery school all the stories and the music are about animals. He hates music anyway.

DR. B.: What is he so afraid they're going to do to him?

MOTHER: Oh, they're going to chase him.

DR. B.: And if they catch him, what will they do to him?

MOTHER: They're going to bite him.

DR. B.: Where?

MOTHER: I don't think I've ever heard him specify.

DR. B.: Have you asked him?

MOTHER: No.

DR. B.: Then why should he specify?

MOTHER: It just never occured to me to ask.

DR. B.: But wouldn't you be interested?

MOTHER: Well . . .

DR. B.: Now think a minute. If a child runs up to you and says, "A dog bit me," first of all you would ask——

MOTHER: Yes, "Where did he bite you?"

DR. B.: All right. So you see, you don't take his fantasy as seriously as reality. Now, if you want to help him with his fears or his fearful fantasies, you have to treat them as seriously as reality. And in reality if your child said, "I've been bitten," you would ask, "Where?" You'd get down to specifics.

MOTHER: Well, suppose I find out where he's afraid he'll be bitten.

DR. B.: If he tells you.

MOTHER: Yes, if he tells me. Do yōu think he knows?

DR. B.: No. And I don't think he'll necessarily tell you the truth. Certainly if he says things that sound improbable to me I wouldn't fall for it. I'd go on with the questions for a while. But there only your intuition can tell you when to stop.

MOTHER: Well, should I start with some reassurance?

DR. B.: No. I think if you give that too early, the child gets alarmed. "My God! Mommy thinks I need reassurance with that. If I were to tell her the true thing, what would she think?" That's often what happens when reassurance is given like a patent medicine. You take it out like a Band-Aid, pop it on, and that's that. But if it's really a deep-seated fear, the child won't tell you right away, not the real thing. He'll watch you. From what you tell me of his looking forward to Thanksgiving, he was already testing you with the turkey. "Would even *my* mommy cut the turkey's head off, or will she be the one who'll let the turkey live?" But hindsight is always easy. I probably wouldn't have known what was behind all this either, at the moment. After all, the child goes to nursery school, he hears about Thanksgiving, and so on. But what about his other fears; before this business set in?

SECOND MOTHER: Can I ask ... why do you make him keep going to nursery school?

MOTHER: I don't. I'm removing him next quarter. The reason I urged him to go was because of his little sister. She's a year and a half, and he has a hard time ever playing unmolested by her. All day long there's this constant interchange, and it's very bad for both of them. I thought if he could have a little peace ... But of course if he's not getting any peace out of nursery school either ...

DR. B.: What's his relationship to his sister otherwise?

MOTHER: It's mixed.

DR. B.: And what does he think in general about his being a boy?

MOTHER: Well, you remember about a year ago, we had that little talk about him?

DR. B.: Can you remind me?

MOTHER: There was a period there when he wanted to be a girl.

DR. B.: I think he's not through with that period, yet.

MOTHER: Oh, I see what you mean. Well, he started out by announcing that he wanted to sit on the toilet like a girl, and a little later he specified that he wanted to be like a girl.

DR. B.: In which way?

MOTHER: Oh, various things. He thought dresses were prettier than overalls, for instance.

DR. B.: Did you discuss with him the difference between boys and girls, and the sitting down on the toilet? Yes ... I remember now. We did discuss it. Well, how did he take it?

MOTHER: I think it went very well.

DR. B.: Well, maybe it went too fast and now we get the backwash.

MOTHER: Maybe so. Because recently the question's come up again a couple of times, the way it did the original time; of whether or not all babies were girls, and then after a while they turned into boys.

DR. B.: And whether they turn back into girls again if they misbehave. Well, how does he feel now, about his penis?

MOTHER: He hasn't mentioned it in a long time.

DR. B.: Then I would talk about it, I think.

MOTHER: How do you mean?

DR. B.: Well, I think he has certain anxieties; it's very hard to say what about, it can be so many things. You blame the nursery school. But the fact remains that there were fifteen or twenty other children in his class who did not develop the same anxiety, who did not develop the same aversion to songs about animals; and having known you for several years, I'm not willing to believe that the other children's mothers are better mothers.

MOTHER: No, I don't say it was the nursery that precipitated things. I know there was enough basis for this kind of anxiety before. All he needed was something to set him off.

SECOND MOTHER: Dr. Bettelheim, what about this discovery that we eat animals and fish and so on? Is it likely, or unlikely, that most children, when they discover this concept, at whatever age, wouldn't be bothered by it to some extent?

DR. B.: Look, you ask me to generalize and I hate to generalize. Some do, and some don't. I think it's probably upsetting to every child. But then he has many upsetting experiences. It all depends on what he connects it with, and at what moment it hits him.

SECOND MOTHER: And then that gives you the answer in terms of his anxiety?

DR. B.: Yes, if you know the moment when it really hits him. Because you might get it weeks and months later—and that's what we're groping for at this moment. When did this hit him and then combine with and aggravate his other anxieties? Tell me, does he really reject fish and chicken? And what is really his expression? How does he react to it when he's eating?

MOTHER: Oh, he eats it now, but there were a couple of weeks when he wouldn't.

DR. B.: And how did you handle that?

MOTHER: I didn't say anything.

DR. B.: And he wouldn't eat it?

MOTHER: He wouldn't touch it!

DR. B.: And did you discuss with him why?

MOTHER: No. I assumed the reason was that he thought I killed it.

DR. B.: Ah! You assume too much, my girl. Even if your assumption is correct, it's no good. Here he does something unusual and it must be so bad that mommy doesn't even talk about it.

MOTHER: Well, that's the truth. I know I don't want to talk about it. I'm too anxious about it to know how to deal with it.

DR. B.: That's right. But why are you so anxious about it? You've been eating chicken all your life.

MOTHER: Yes, but I'm just anxious about his general reaction to the knowledge of the killing. Well, I don't know. Here all this time we've been reading him stories about the nice friendly ducks and the chickens, how they act just like people, or feel just like people. And now we're going to tell him that we go out and cut their heads off and eat them up.

DR. B.: Very true, very true.

MOTHER: I wish now I'd never read him such stories. Then I wouldn't be so worried about it. But I can see the connection myself. They've been treated just like people in all the stories we read, and if you kill them, why don't you go out and kill people?

DR. B.: Yes, but where did he get the idea that we kill people?

MOTHER: He doesn't get it yet, but I do!

DR. B.: No, no! Don't make a little angel out of your boy. The idea of killing, of doing away and all that, by now it's right there in his own head. But let's find out why you're so worried about these chicken and turkeys and fish. The fish don't talk in the story.

MOTHER: Oh, no! But there are songs!

DR. B.: Some, but not that many. You see, you overlook something. To you these animals are nice animals and they talk like human beings, but the distance between them and human beings is much greater in your head than in his. Or to put it the other way around—he would think much less of doing away with, or killing, another child—

MOTHER: Than I would!

DR. B.: That's right! So we have to ask ourselves how much of all this anxiety about doing away with something living comes from you and how much comes from him.

MOTHER: As a matter of fact, I wouldn't be surprised if a lot of his general insecurity about violence in all forms comes from my own anxiety. I know it showed up at a very early age.

DR. B.: And then let's have a little talk about the atomic bomb in the family, and we wonder why the children are anxious. It's not the talk about the bomb. After all, what does the bomb mean to a child? But the frightful anxiety when we talk about it. Now let's go back to the music, which interested me. Why do you think he reacted so to the music?

MOTHER: Oh, he's always had a kind of reaction to music. When he was much younger he liked it for about half an hour and then he would insist we turn it off; he didn't want that noise any more. Then there was the business when he broke his phonograph. He broke it not once, but two or three times.

DR. B.: Now, didn't it occur to you that this was something much more talking than the animals you read about? Something talking and therefore human?

MOTHER: No, . . . it didn't occur to me.

DR. B.: And what did he break off?

MOTHER: The arm . . . and he got very upset about it. For a while he wouldn't listen to any music at all.

DR. B.: That's right. So there you have one of the origins of his fear of violence. Here's something that really talks, and talks pleasantly. You jerk something off—an attachment, a gadget—and the music stops. It stops talking. "I killed the noise. I'm a killer."

SECOND MOTHER: How can you live in this world!

DR. B.: No. The real point is that if your child weren't already acutely anxious about something, he wouldn't have established such a connection. After all, these things happen and children break things. My question about the music was just chance. But now we see that it was the first killing of the voice or of a sound-making thing, just as animals make sounds. And probably if we went on there would be more things. I think that with many repetitions of such experiences, and the erroneous ideas children harbor about them, things can go wrong. Our only chance of avoiding any cumulative effect is to talk about it each time. We'll never catch all their wrong interpretations. But we can catch a lot, and it's our only chance. Shall we go on, or are you all exhausted with this?

MOTHER: It's a big subject ... I'm only beginning to realize it. Partly, it's that a number of his anxieties have converged.

DR. B.: That's right! And I think that what has most converged is that this boy is very much attached to you, would like very much to make your standards of nonviolence his own, but yet he has a lot of violence in himself. Do you see what I mean? And unless you give some approval to some of his violence ...

MOTHER: Well, what can I do? The main problem we have is with his sister. He very rarely attacks her without provocation, but it doesn't take much provocation.

DR. B.: And what do you do?

MOTHER: I tell him over and over again that he mustn't do that; that if she bothers him he must tell me and I will take her away.

DR. B.: Take her away where?

MOTHER: To another room.

DR. B.: Yes, but what do you actually tell him?

MOTHER: I think I say ... that I will take her away. But I never do.

DR. B.: Not only that ...

MOTHER: Oh ...

DR. B.: How can he tell on her if you make such a threat to her very existence?

61

MOTHER: Good heavens!

DR. B.: You see, you take for granted that his thinking proceeds along the same line of verbal usage as yours. But small children are very literal. You "will take her away" means exactly that, and not that you will put her in another room.

SECOND MOTHER: "Hold your horses" means to hold horses!

DR. B.: Exactly! And how can you hold horses if you don't have horses to hold? To "pipe down" means you have a pipe in your mouth and you put the pipe down.

MOTHER: Well, what do I do now? Is it too late?

DR. B.: No, it isn't too late. Don't give me this "too late" business. It's never too late to correct things. But I do think it's not only this "take away" business; it's more than that. I think you expect too much of him, to expect that he should really be able, when he's angry, to wait and tell you. So it's not only that you threaten the sister; because if you take the sister away for misbehaving (when after all she's just a baby and unreasonable), what will you do to him if he misbehaves (he who is older and should know better)?

MOTHER: Well, what should I do? I can't let him hurt her. And he does sometimes.

DR. B.: No, but I think you should take his part more, and we've discussed this before, I think you should agree with him that she's a terrible bother and it's very hard to be a reasonable, law-abiding citizen of three with such an unsocialized little sister. It's really a very tough fate, and I would commiserate with him. But also tell him that there's nothing we can do. We just have to live through it. We cannot take her away. We cannot send her away. And you'll have to insist on the permanence of the present arrangement; that no wishes and no anxiety will change it. The baby is here to stay, and she's here to stay as a girl. And he is here to stay, and he's here to stay as a boy.

MOTHER: Just to keep saying it.

DR. B.: You cannot say it often enough, in all the variations. That he was born with all parts of his body. He has them now and will have them all his life. And then if he goes down the street and sees a man who's lost an arm he'll probably have all the fears he started out with. Still, mommy's word will have to carry more reassurance than the world of reality. Because if you start out with "Some people in this world lose an arm," then we're right back where we started from. Let him deny it; let him repress it—even what he's seen with his own eyes. He's still better off. But what do we do with mommy's fears about her own aggressions? That's where we cannot quite separate your intense inner disapproval of hostility and aggression from your child's fears.

MOTHER: I know one thing ... that when I correct with intense inner disapproval, or shout at him, or get angry with him ... I'm immediately overwhelmed with guilt feelings.

DR. B.: That's right. Well, I think we understand one another so far. Let's come back to it again in two weeks.

[Two weeks later]

MOTHER: I want to report something of what happened to us. You remember last time ... you suggested I should commiserate with my older boy?

DR. B.: Yes, that's always good.

MOTHER: Well, it worked beautifully!

DR. B.: Don't tell me! Aren't we astonished!

MOTHER: Well, *I* was! I was astonished at the improvement in their relationship, because it works both ways. I mean, it gives him an opportunity to feel patronizing and a little patient with her. And this makes her a little less grabby and bothersome.

DR. B.: Oh, of course it helps. But it doesn't solve things.

63

MOTHER: Oh, no, it doesn't solve it. They still have fights. But not quite so often. Furthermore it gives me a little warning. I mean, I begin to hear him say, "No, Peggy, we don't do that ... that's not the way I want to play." Well, you see, that gives me time to get there. Whereas, if all I hear is "No!" [slap!] before I get there ... [Burst of laughter]

DR. B.: But now you know the great secret of education. Just involve the students in discussion while you gain time to think out your answers. Well, I'm very happy at what you've told me.

[The above interchange took place close to the beginning of the session. The mother spoke freely about her success in helping her son hold his own against his little sister. Sorting out her own feelings about violence was a much harder task. About an hour later she began to speak again, at first with a great deal of hesitation.]

MOTHER: Dr. Bettelheim . . . do you remember the long conversation we had the last time? Well, after I got home I thought of the thing you were probably looking for ... the incident ... all the time. I don't know why I didn't think of it here ... but ... the incident of breaking the record player coincided very closely with his having to be taken to the doctor to have his foreskin pulled back. It had become adhesed. And it all happened shortly after Peggy was born. It even connects with this worry about the chickens with their heads cut off. Because after I remembered the incident I remembered that ... well, in the first place we had to help the doctor. That is, we had to hold him down. And in the second place, when we got through the doctor explained to me, "Now, be very careful. Every day, when you clean it, pull it back completely, so that the head is exposed." Well, once I remembered that, I also realized that although I tried to reassure him at the time, I didn't reassure him correctly. That is, what probably worried him was that he was damaged in some way.

DR. B.: And what's going to be cut off next?

MOTHER: That's right. Now shortly after that, something else came up that I realize I'm going to have to face sooner or later. He was out one day with a couple of other children; another mother had taken her child and a few others to the lake, to go wading. And the mother had a little boy just about Tom's age who was circumcised. So when they were getting undressed the little boy looked at Tom's penis and said, "What's the matter with his penis, it's not a bit like mine?" Well, the mother didn't answer, since it wasn't her child. She just reported the incident to me but she wasn't sure if Tom had heard it. Well, Tom's never mentioned it or brought it up, but sooner or later he's going to, I'm sure. Now, what do I say?

DR. B.: What interests me first, before we go into that, is, how come it didn't occur to you while we were talking? When did it occur to you?

MOTHER: It occurred to me shortly after I left here. But I know why it didn't occur to me sooner. I was too concerned with something else the whole time I was talking to you. I was following a line of thought of my own that interfered . . .

DR. B.: Namely?

MOTHER: With thinking about what I knew, you were trying to make me think about. Well, mainly, I felt sure . . . I felt so guilty about his various anxieties . . . thinking how they were directly the result of all the times I've been angry with him, or hit him, or something like that. I was so anxious to get that part out, that I didn't concentrate on the other part.

DR. B.: I'm glad you said that, because this is something very important. I don't know if all of you here tonight were present last time. But I think it's one of the most important matters we can discuss. I'm talking about how our own private guilt feelings may have no connection at all with what's troubling a child. This prevents us from doing the right thing with and for the child.

It isn't that we couldn't see. Because with children, particularly young children, things are usually pretty simple. What interferes is our own involvement—either the kind of child we want to have, the guilt we feel about something, and so forth. But it's something we must learn to recognize. If we have done something wrong and feel guilty about it, we must be careful not to get mixed up and think that must also be the cause of what then happens with the child. Usually it's not, and for a very simple reason. Because our thinking, our guilt or emotional involvement, proceeds on a much more rarified plane of morality, particularly among educated groups.

Things that greatly concern us are usually way beyond the child's level of experience. His is much simpler, and connections are established, for example, between direct visual experiences of bodily harm; things we don't even think about or that we know well have nothing to do with each other. All of which then interferes with our assessing correctly what goes on in the child's mind. Fortunately, the reassurance a child needs is again simpler, for the same reasons.

To your boy, for example, the penis, at least as a sex organ, has no particularly greater meaning than any other part of the body. Therefore, when you talk to the child, the main thing is not to get too involved in your own involvement in sex and what sex means to you.

Now, circumcision, it's true, isn't easy to explain to a child. What I'd try to do is to find an innocuous but comparable example of medical treatment. Don't say, "It doesn't hurt." Sometimes parents compare it to the cutting off of nails or hair, and insist it doesn't hurt. Don't ever do that, because it's an invitation for the children to try to find out, and then you're in a big mess. Because it hurts, and it hurts badly. Some minor surgery, if there's been any, would be comparable. But the main thing is for the parent not to make a special fuss because it's the penis. That's all the advice I can give you. Say, "Yes, it was necessary for the doctor to fix something, but now it's all fixed and it's over."

MOTHER: Well, Tom was sore for about ten days, and that was how the trouble started.

DR. B.: I know, and usually I don't like lies. But rather than get involved in a discussion of circumcision with a child of three or four, I would just say, "Yes, penises come in different sizes and different forms. Sure, different boys have different-looking penises."

MOTHER: It's not a lie, is it?

DR. B.: Yes, it is a lie, let's face it. But I'm willing, up to the age of six or seven or eight, until verbal communication is better established, to just put it on the basis of bodily differences. Instead of saying, "Yes, the other boy had a foreskin, and it was cut off," I'd just say, "Yes, they're different." Some have this foreskin and it's big and covers the glans or the head, and where the foreskin is short it doesn't cover it.

But do you see the point I was trying to make? I can't help you very much with your concrete problem. But what a wild goose chase we were drawn on because you started out with pacifism and brotherly love, when what was actually bothering your son was the consequence of adhesions of the foreskin. As you see, this can effectively blind you to very simple matters. We could otherwise have given the child simple reassurance and resolved a concrete anxiety before it got all tangled up with not eating meat and other extraneous matters.

II

Their Problem or Ours?

1

Learning for What?

MOTHER: I have a question. My son is a year and a half now and he's talking very well. His vocabulary is well over 150 words and he has a word for just about everything he can touch on his body except for his genitals. We haven't given him a word for that yet. Now what should we do? My husband says we should tell him.

DR. B.: Why? Has the question come up?

MOTHER: No, he hasn't said, "What's that?" but he comes up with other questions and I don't know when he'll ask about this.

DR. B.: I really don't know, and I don't know why you're worried about it. But I am worried about your being worried.

MOTHER: Well, it really doesn't bother me too much, except that it's a gap in his vocabulary. He knows "leg," and "hand," and "finger." He knows all that.

SECOND MOTHER: The same with my little boy. He has a doll, and he goes through all the parts of the doll and names them. But when he comes to the penis, the doll doesn't have one, and then he looks up at me.

DR. B.: Well, I must say the families your youngsters are growing up in are different. The kids on the street would find this very funny.

MOTHER: Oh, they'll pick up the other words on the street, anyway.

DR. B.: Then they'll have a double-standard vocabulary.

MOTHER: Yes, but then that will establish a difference between me and his friends.

DR. B.: Oh, I think the fact that you even want to teach him the word establishes the difference, don't you? So what are you worried about? Frankly, I'm more interested in your counting his vocabulary.

MOTHER: Oh, he learns new words every day, at least two a day. I've got a whole list of them! I send his new words to his grandmothers.

DR. B.: So that's why he has to learn the word "penis"! Well, I doubt that his learning it will make the grandmothers very happy. But okay, it's easy to make fun of such a matter, but it's serious too. And I'm seriously interested in why you count your son's vocabulary.

MOTHER: Because it's a matter of pride. He catches on so fast.

DR. B.: Well now, that you take pleasure at his catching on fast, that's fine.

MOTHER: We do!

DR. B.: That's all right. But the counting; why do you count the words? And the reporting to grandmother.

MOTHER: Well, they're so far away and they want to know.

DR. B.: Oh, I grant you that writing to grandparents can be a problem. Many parents know lots of stories about their children, but when it comes to writing to the grandmother, none of them come to mind. Then it's blank. But they know they have to write and they want to amuse their parents with appealing stories about their children. It isn't that grandmother isn't nice about it. But some parents just have a resistance, you know, to using their children for this purpose. Others don't have this resistance and they think it's the right thing to do. But I'm just a little afraid that you may be pushing him. I don't say you're actually pushing, but he might feel he's being pushed.

MOTHER: Then I shouldn't give him the word until he wants it.

DR. B.: No, you shouldn't give him any word! I would rather you just talk to him.

MOTHER: Oh, we do!

DR. B.: I know you do. But I think he should pick the words up on his own, make his own selection from what you say when you're talking to him.

MOTHER: I think he does that.

DR. B.: I'm sure he does. He must. Otherwise, how did he start? But you see your statement was about "a list of 150 words"; and you specify his learning two new words every day. So while I don't believe that's exactly so—

MOTHER: But they're all written down!

DR. B.: All right, all the more so! I suggest you forget about recording the new words.

MOTHER: Well, they accumulate so fast. As soon as I notice that he says "ham" . . .

DR. B.: What?

MOTHER: For lunch—ham—well, then I say, "Ah, you can say that now," and that's the end of it.

DR. B.: Well, I wouldn't be so sure that's the end of it.

MOTHER: I don't always, but if my husband is with me, then I point it out.

SECOND MOTHER: I do that, too. Tonight, for example, my son said "dessert" for the first time, and I said to my husband, "Oh, he said 'dessert.'"

MOTHER: Mine's been saying that for a long time.

SECOND MOTHER: Oh, but this was *my* son, and he's even younger!

DR.B.: Well, there I'm caught. It's yes and no. I'm caught because I seem to contradict myself. I am not against what you [*to the second mother*] are doing.

SECOND MOTHER: Well then, I don't understand your point.

DR. B.: The point is that I'm not against approval,

73

and certainly not against your enjoying that he's learned a new word. The child should gain approval for his achievements—that's good and it's necessary, because otherwise no child would learn. Why should he? But while I think the child should get approval and recognition for his achievements, I get worried when I have the feeling it's expected of him.

MOTHER: Oh, I see. But it isn't at all like that!

DR. B.: Well, I didn't say it was. But the way you talk about it put the doubt in my head, which may by no means be justified.

MOTHER: Well, people doubted our statement that he was learning two words a day. So I just watched him to check on myself, to see if I was wrong. And I wasn't; I know it!

DR. B.: Yes, I know. Some children are very bright, and yours sounds like a bright child. I think there's nothing wrong in his learning words like that. What I am worried about is that a pattern can be established, that the child may feel an obligation——

MOTHER: Of pushing?

DR. B.: No, but a sense of obligation, which is very different from a parent pushing the child.

MOTHER: You mean he gets the notion ... he feels that I'm expecting something ... *éclatant!*

DR. B.: Exactly! And that's what grandmothers expect, too.

MOTHER: Yes.

DR. B.: Do you see now what worried me? Because then the poor child has no choice but to meet your expectations. Yet learning should be a more spontaneous thing. For what he has learned on his own he should get ample praise. Otherwise we get this quiz-kid stuff, or the spelling-bee stuff, where the kids spell words they don't really know how to use and it's not part of their living vocabulary. Especially at this age, words have a very magical connotation and we have to be a bit careful. The child thinks he has mastered—and he really has—something he can use. He's really achieved something because he can now tell you he wants dessert. But if it isn't really something he can use for himself, that's another story. It's hard to explain. Do you know what I mean?

MOTHER: No.

DR. B.: Well, let me put it this way. It's a fact in our society that you can get very far if you can talk well and fast. And there are many successful, even famous, people who get far because they're glib. But if their talk has little resemblance to their actions, they're not very useful members of society, and usually they're not very happy. You can even find them in the universities! And this is where approval comes in. I'm afraid there's too much approval and push on the verbal achievement, and not an equal concern for how it relates to one's life. Do you see what I mean?

Now, I don't accuse you, and I don't even suspect you of doing this in fact. But your statement made me fear that you might, and so I thought we should talk about it. Is that clear to all of you? After all, it's tricky, because we must encourage our children to talk. We must encourage them to learn, to increase their vocabulary. But it seems to me that the way to do it is to talk with them more and more, to talk about what's important to them, and to see that they respond— rather than just stressing the learning of words.

MOTHER: I don't know. It seems to me that he's already so delighted with the actual learning of words. He says something to me and I can't get it, and then he repeats it and I do, and he goes "Ah!" And he's happy about it!

DR. B.: Oh, sure! That's all right. I'm not talking about the child's part in this, you know. The child must feel really good about learning new words, about learning to talk in sentences. That's really an achievement. But it should be an enjoyment that comes about naturally. And for us it should very definitely be an enjoyment because the child has mastered something he wanted to achieve, and *not,* "I have such a bright child!" Do you see? Everything along the first line of feeling is fine ... any intensity or degree. But even the smallest degree of the latter can be damaging. [*Mother laughs*]

DR. B.: Why do you laugh?

MOTHER: Because I've just accepted the fact that my kid is a genius! I don't even think about it any more!

SECOND MOTHER: He thinks she's kidding!

DR. B.: Well, the main thing is that he doesn't begin to feel that to win his mother's love he has to be a genius with words.... Now ... if we're finished with this, we have time for one or two more questions.

[*Attention now shifted to another mother, who wondered about children floating toys in the toilet bowl. Did that mean they were getting ready for toilet training? After a brief discussion the first mother spoke up again.*]

MOTHER: My boy loves to play in the toilet bowl, too, and then flush the toilet. Do you think I should start toilet training him?

DR. B.: How old, again?

MOTHER: Almost nineteen months.

DR. B.: I think you might suggest it. After all, he has quite a vocabulary. What do the two of you do with your 150-word vocabulary?

MOTHER: Oh, we talk about toys, people.

DR. B.: And sometimes the political situation?

MOTHER: Almost.

DR. B.: Well, that takes us back to what I meant by a living vocabulary. This vocabulary you must now put to use in living.

MOTHER: Well, I don't know ... how would you tell him "before"? I don't know if he has that in his vocabulary. And I thought you said that at seventeen months or so they were too young to train.

DR. B.: No, I never said so. I didn't say you should feel compelled to establish it at seventeen or nineteen months, but you can very well suggest it! There's nothing wrong with explaining it to your child if his vocabulary permits you to do it so he can understand you. And if his reaction is "No," then it's "No," and that's all there is to it.

MOTHER: Well, is there any attitude you would suggest we have toward it?

DR. B.: Well, now, look! On the one hand we're so happy if he learns to say "dessert," and you also want to give him the right word for penis. After all, neither of those is a very great achievement, whereas toilet training is an honest to goodness social advance. So why don't you set his great intellectual abilities to work toward real social achievements?

MOTHER: Well, because I'm sure the word "before" has no meaning to him! And if I say, "Tell Mommy before you do it," it won't mean anything to him.

DR. B.: That's perfectly true. Say, "Do it *there!*" [*Burst of laughter*] Tell him, "That goes *there!*" And point, in case he doesn't understand, "there." At that age you can't explain "before." If they did understand "before" and "after," I really would be surprised if toilet training hadn't already developed. Because those are complicated concepts. But for toilet training all you need to know is where it belongs. After all, they know that for sleeping they belong in bed at night.

SECOND MOTHER: Doctor Bettelheim, I've never understood clearly at what age you start to "suggest" it to them.

DR. B.: When they have enough of a vocabulary to understand what you want. Certainly not before. When they can safely sit up and have relative control of their muscles, and not before. Because you must have muscle control to sit safely on the potty or toilet seat. Then you can suggest it. And if they say "No," it's "No." Then maybe two months later you suggest it again; and this game you play up to the age of three.

MOTHER: Well, you said last summer that we shouldn't begin training a few months before or after a trip, and we have a trip coming up in a few months.

DR. B.: Oh, I wasn't talking about the kind of training where you say, "This goes there." But I'm glad you bring it up because we can never talk specifically enough. What I meant then by toilet training is where you take the child—when you know the child is going to have a bowel movement—and set him on the toilet. That's what is popularly called "toilet training," and that I'm against. Because what I want to see offered to the child is a learning experience, not the imposing of a conditioned response. Do you see what I mean?

MOTHER: And they'd have to be able to talk, then, before they could do that. And if they want the new experience, they take it.

DR. B.: Yes, that's it. So you see, there are various ways to toilet train a child. Unfortunately, the popular way is to take the child and put it on the toilet, which is something you impose. But basically, the child is then getting two experiences that are really contradictory. The first learning experience is that you take and put him on the toilet. And the second is that he has his movement on the toilet.

Now, the first event cannot go on the rest of his life. Some time he has to learn to go spontaneously. Therefore, I'm all for waiting until the child has shown by other actions that he can spontaneously go someplace and do something. So, for the real learning of toilet training there must be communication, there must be muscular control, there must be evidence that the child knows what it's all about, and there must be evidence that the child can spontaneously go somewhere and do something purposeful, or relatively purposeful. If all that is present, then is the time to "suggest" to the child. Because then, if the child is ready, he is good and ready for it. And if he's not ready, he can say, "No."

MOTHER: I see. I guess I had no plans because I haven't ever thought about it. The word "before" bothered me.

DR. B.: Well, you know, most of the time toilet training is conveyed to the child by putting him on the toilet and making grunting noises. And it isn't such a bad way if you want to do it fast. But you obviously have a very advanced child, who is anxious to learn. So we come back to my original point: let the other learning, the social learning, be commensurate with the intellectual learning, and let both be spontaneous. Does that answer your question?

MOTHER: Yes, now I understand.

2

The Letter

MOTHER: Dr. Bettelheim, what if you have difficulty getting a child to take a bath or go to bed. Is it all right to offer them another toy, or suggest doing something that'll interest them? I thought that would be considered bribery.

DR. B.: What's wrong with bribery?

MOTHER: I don't know.

DR. B.: Well, you said, "It's considered bribery." What's wrong with it?

SECOND MOTHER: I don't know, but it works!

THIRD MOTHER: I'm interested in this, too.

DR. B.: Okay, what about bribery?

SECOND MOTHER: I think it's fine.

DR. B.: I'm not so sure.

SECOND MOTHER: Well, think of it like this. If he's wrapped up in something he can't take to bed, offer him something else.

DR. B.: Ah, but she didn't say that. She thinks it's bribery. Now can you really offer a toy in good faith when you think it's bribing the child? Sure, I can make a very good case for bribery, and one against it, too. Sometimes it's fun to match wits, and I like to do it. But let's ask ourselves, "Can I as a parent really make a case for it if it's bribery?"

THIRD MOTHER: Well, couldn't you just call it a transition?

DR. B.: You can call it anything you want to, but

then you're only trying to fool yourself by giving it a more acceptable name.

SECOND MOTHER: Well, sometimes when Sally doesn't want to take a nap, I feel I'd like to take a nap myself, and if I had a dolly I'd like to go to bed with it. By that time I'm almost convinced that she'd just as soon do that instead of what she is doing. So when I offer her the doll, that's fine.

DR. B.: And do you have the feeling that what you're doing is bribery?

SECOND MOTHER: Well, I don't like that word myself.

DR. B.: But have you ever thought of it as bribery?

SECOND MOTHER: No.

DR. B.: All right. Then you have no problem. But this mother does have a problem because she thinks it's bribery, and I want to know why she thinks so. That's why I'm still on it.

THIRD MOTHER: Because the women's magazines print articles about it.

DR. B.: Well, now, look! I'm in enough trouble without adding the women's magazines at this moment!

MOTHER: I always thought one could use a toy that way, to distract attention.

DR. B.: Why do you want to distract a child's attention?

MOTHER: Well, I mean . . . from something the child is interested in . . . and you want to get him into the tub or to bed. So you give him a toy to distract him. Well, you could say, "bribery."

DR. B.: But the point I'm trying to make is that it makes all the difference in the world whether you yourself think of it as bribery, whatever you actually call it. That is the essence. I'm willing to discuss the issue of bribery on its merits. But I think the broader issue is whether you think of it as bribery. If you feel it's a trick, something amoral, then you really shouldn't do it.

81

MOTHER: Oh, it never entered my head it was that bad.

DR. B.: Well, no. I didn't say it was bad. But you can't deny that a bribe, in common language usage, is something amoral, something not very nice. Correct? Now, do you really think a mother should do something to her child that she doesn't think is very nice?

MOTHER: Oh, no. But what I mean is . . . if she could look at it . . .

DR. B.: Do you really not understand what I'm driving at?

MOTHER: Not very clearly.

SECOND MOTHER: I do. It's "the letter" again.

DR. B.: That's right, it's "the letter" again. "It all depends on how you read the letter."[1] And if you

---

1. "The letter" refers to a story I used repeatedly to illustrate that the actual content of a message is often of little importance compared with the spirit it's received in.

The story is much better told than read, since the entire point rests on emotional emphasis used in the telling. It goes as follows. A letter arrives from the son of the family who is away at college. The father opens it, reads it, and throws it on the table angrily, saying, "I'll be damned if I send him money if that's the way he's going to ask for it!" The mother asks anxiously, "Goodness, what did he write?" and the father reads, in a gruff voice, "Dear *Father*, I'm *broke*; please send me some money *immediately*. Your *son*." The mother picks the letter up, reads it, and shakes her head, saying, "I can't see anything wrong with the letter. It's a very nice letter," and she reads in tones of affection: "*Dear* Father, I'm broke; *please* send me *some* money immediately. *Your* son." To which the father replies, "Ah, that's another story. If the poor guy's broke and needs money, let's send him some."

I used this example whenever mothers spoke of seeming inconsistencies in my advice, such as telling one mother to go ahead with a certain practice while asking another mother using the same practice to examine her purpose and feelings carefully. The reasons for the inconsistency were usually the same: I knew the mothers fairly well by that time, and I knew from past interchange that in the first case the mother felt quite comfortable about engaging in the practice, while the second mother harbored opposite feelings about the identical situation. Thus, my allusion read it the wrong way—even if it's the right letter from my point of view—if it's the wrong letter from the mother's point of view, it's still the wrong letter. It will neither achieve its purpose nor be good. Now then, we can go to the second question: what is bribery? First we have to decide if we consider something bribery. If so, then we shouldn't do it, even if it may be a short cut. Because after all, that's what a bribe is—a short cut, an avoidance of difficulties. And after we've agreed that bribery is bad, but that a certain action in our eyes is not bribery, let's find out why in this mother's eyes such behavior is bribery. Do you see what I mean? Okay, you've got the floor.

MOTHER: Well, I don't know. At first I did it, and I never thought of it as bribery. It was just a way of distracting her and asking her to come. But later on . . . I don't know . . .

DR. B.: How did it creep in?

MOTHER: I don't know. It happened in about the last three weeks, or a month. She'd be playing there happily . . . and she doesn't particularly want to take her nap . . .

DR. B.: How old?

MOTHER: She'll be twenty-one months. And suddenly I find it very difficult, where I didn't before, so I offer her something else. And while I'm doing it I'm not conscious of the fact that it's bribery. But after she has it and seems happy, I do think it.

DR.B.: Why?

MOTHER: I really don't know why.

DR. B.: I think you should take a little counsel with yourself and find out why. How come you don't say, "Well, now she has to take a nap, and by golly I'm going to make it just as pleasant for her as I know

to the story of the letter meant: we cannot judge the merit of an action on the basis of appearance alone, but must consider the context of feelings and values within which it takes place.

how. If I want her to take a nap, then the least I can do is to make it as pleasant as possible."

MOTHER: That's right, make her happier.

DR. B.: Yes. But if you really thought that way, you would never call it bribery. You would just consider it the obligation of a mother who knows what is hard and what is easy for a child, and who knows how to make it easier. You would consider it the normal obligation of an intelligent parent to make things easy for his child where he can. But why you should call it bribery, I don't know.

FOURTH MOTHER: I wonder. I know what my own experience has been . . . and I wonder if she isn't feeling guilty about making the child nap because *she* wants the quiet, and because of that she feels she's bullying the child into something.

DR. B.: Yes! That's exactly what I was driving at! You know that the child needs her nap. But you also know that you want some rest. And feeling guilty because you want to rest, too, you conclude that that's no reason why the child should take a nap. So it's the knowledge that it's you who wants something for yourself that makes you feel guilty when you try to get the kid to take a nap. Then, if you do get her to bed by offering a toy you're afraid something's wrong, and you think that what's wrong is the bribery. In short, you extend the guilt feeling about wanting her to nap onto offering her a toy to make napping easier. But there's no reason to feel guilty for either of the two; on the contrary. There is certainly nothing wrong in wanting something for yourself. My suggestion is that you start out by thinking, "I need some rest; if I can now get her to take a nap, we can both have our rest and then we'll both be better off." So the issue of bribery came about because you felt it was wrong to want some rest. But I believe that deep down you can't give your child a good rest if you can't permit yourself some when you need it.

To believe that we have no rights just because we've become parents is nearly as bad as the antiquated notion that our children have no rights because they're ours to do with as we see fit. I think the first notion is one of those erroneous ideas that has crept in with that other one, "We must do what the child wants at the moment he wants it." After all, you're an adult, and the supposition is that you know a bit more than a twenty-one-month-old child what is good for her. I know there are those who hold that a child should be allowed to do exactly as he pleases. Well, I don't agree. But I do think we should see to it that he can always do what is best for him. And to have a good rest by getting him to bed without a fight because you've distracted him or offered him a nice toy—that's good for him.

FOURTH MOTHER: But you don't, though, think a child should be forced to sleep?

DR. B.: You *can't* force a child to sleep. So we'd better try to make it attractive.

3

Rebel in Overalls

MOTHER: Dr. Bettelheim, I was wondering how much a child of three should be encouraged to ... in her ... the only way I can think of it is in terms of femininity. Just lately she wants very much to wear dresses. She's very much aware of the word "pretty" and the reason she wants to wear dresses is because she thinks they're prettier than overalls.

DR. B.: And who gave her this idea?

MOTHER: Well, she ... it's because there's no doubt that she ... every girl child does look better in a dress than in overalls, and when she does wear a dress the neighbors will remark on it.

DR. B.: So it's the neighbors who gave her the idea.

MOTHER: Yes. Adults will remark.

DR. B.: Because the idea of "pretty" and of dress must come from somewhere. They don't develop that spontaneously.

MOTHER: Well, I've never tried to give her the concept at all because I don't know if it should be encouraged or not.

DR. B.: That depends on what kind of a child you want.

MOTHER: Well, I don't want a child that's aware of clothes to the extent that I've seen it in some children— where they'll throw a tantrum if the ribbons don't match the dress, and they have to choose their own dress. On the other hand—

DR. B.: Would you rather she threw a tantrum because you're a bad mother? A three-year-old will throw tantrums from time to time, and sometimes the ribbons are just a convenient excuse.

MOTHER: Yes, but sometimes not. Sometimes they've become so clothes-conscious——

DR. B.: That's right. But my point is, let's not jump to conclusions when a three-year-old throws a tantrum if the ribbons don't match. To a large degree it's the child's attempt to be independent and to get his own will. Do you see what I mean? The clothes are a relatively innocuous issue, and I think that any child who is not utterly subdued will, between the ages of two and a half and five, both boys and girls, throw tantrums about what to wear and what not to wear. It has little to do with femininity, but it has a lot to do with their experimenting with independence, with having their own mind, and so on.

MOTHER: Well, that's exactly the point, Dr. Bettelheim, I've tended to discourage the wearing of dresses primarily because I think she'll be more comfortable in overalls. On the other hand, I don't want to stymie any independence of choice she may be wanting to exercise. And then, the third thing is, I don't want her to become aware of the concept of "pretty."

DR. B.: But the neighbors have already done that.

MOTHER: Well, I can stymie it. But I don't know whether . . .

DR. B.: How can you?

MOTHER: By discouraging it.

DR. B.: No, you cannot. How can you discourage it? If the child says that she wants to look pretty, what choice have you?

MOTHER: Well, I can tell her, "You look pretty in overalls."

DR. B.: Does she really?

MOTHER: No-o . . .

DR. B.: All right. Then you'd be lying.

[*A low buzz of comment*]

SECOND MOTHER: Good heavens, what's wrong with the child's wanting to look pretty?

DR. B.: Wait a minute. I'm trying to get to that, but it's a good question.

MOTHER: I didn't even hear it.

SECOND MOTHER: I just said, what's wrong with the child feeling pretty in something.

MOTHER: Well, it's the whole feeling I have that a child shouldn't be aware of things like that.

DR. B. Of what *should* a child be aware?

MOTHER: Oh? . . . in what sense?

DR. B.: I don't know. I'm asking *you*. Since you know what a child should not be aware of, you must also have some notion of what she should be aware of. Do you see what I mean? You can't give me only the negative. Every negative has a positive. You say that a child shouldn't be too aware of clothes. All right. That's an argument I might or might not accept, depending on what you think the child should be aware of.

MOTHER: Oh . . . they should be aware of many things. The relationship to her friends . . .

DR. B.: Is a three-year-old really aware of her relationship to her friends?

MOTHER: I think so. But I think that's going astray. I think the question is quite specific, and I just want to know whether or not to give her this independence of choice, or whether to stymie any attentiveness to it all.

DR. B.: Never stymie anything, period. That's simple. If you give me such a simple question you'll get a simple answer. Only, it won't help you. Because although you ask me, you have very definite opinions. So my answer won't make any difference at all.

MOTHER: But it will make a difference, otherwise it wouldn't have been a question in my mind.

DR. B.: Yes, but the bigger issue is—what do you think are important issues for a girl of three? What would you consider important and legitimate issues for a three-year-old?

MOTHER: What do you mean by issues?

DR. B.: Well, wearing a dress versus overalls is obviously an issue to your child. You say it's not, that you don't want it to be an issue. Okay, what do you want to be an issue?

MOTHER: I want her to be able to choose what things she would like to play with at any specific time, and . . .

DR. B.: Toys, yes, and clothes, no? That doesn't make sense.

MOTHER: Sure it makes sense.

DR. B.: Why? Because again, you seem to have a certain picture of your child as a grown-up person, of what kind of a person you do and don't want her to be. But you haven't come out and told me that, and therefore I'm stuck. [Turning to others] Don't you have this impression . . . that there's a kind of anxiety about, "I don't want my child to grow up to be a clothes-horse," and so on?

SECOND MOTHER: Yes, but isn't it a matter of what are already issues for the child, and what are not? You can't just say this can be, and this can't.

DR. B.: No, of course not. But it's exactly the same with the clothes business. [Turning back to the mother] I think you have very definite ideas, and you're already afraid that if you let your child talk too much about being pretty and about pretty clothes it will have certain consequences later in life.

MOTHER: Well, I'm afraid she'll turn into what I've seen her cousins turning into.

DR. B.: And do the cousins have the same mother that she does?

MOTHER: No, they all have different mothers.

DR. B.: That's right. So why . . .

MOTHER: But they're all . . . this whole . . . I hate to use the word "middle class," but that's what it is!

DR. B.: What's wrong with the middle class?

MOTHER: I mean, for a child to be preoccupied with . . .

DR. B.: Well, what do you want her to be, a proletarian? What *do* you want her to be?

MOTHER: I want her to be a rebel!

[*Some sounds of amusement and amazement*]

DR. B.: Finally! At least we know now what she wants her child to be.

THIRD MOTHER: How do you know she won't rebel against your particular scale of values?

MOTHER: Well, I hope that they're sound enough so that . . .

DR. B.: What do you mean, sound enough? Against what do you rebel?

MOTHER: Against the unfairness of the society we're living in, to a large extent.

DR. B.: It looks to me as if it's been treating you quite fairly, or you wouldn't be sitting here tonight.

MOTHER: Well, I've been fighting it all my life, helping to make it better. I mean, not fighting it, but . . .

DR. B.: How? By wearing overalls?

MOTHER: Well, by trying to make it better in our own way.

SECOND MOTHER: Well . . . I think we all know what associations she's trying to make. The fact that there are certain attitudes that stand for things we object to.

THIRD MOTHER: Yes, but what has that to do with overalls?

MOTHER: Oh, not the overalls but the fact that . . . I feel it, but I can't say it.

THIRD MOTHER: Well, isn't it true that when a child becomes aware of the outside world, his personal belongings become much more important to him, his shoes, his socks, his overalls, and so forth? And I can't see what's wrong with that, or their taking pride in what belongs to them.

DR. B.: What worries me so much more is that this mother, I'm sorry to say, already wants her three-year-old to fight her own battles with society, which doesn't seem right.

MOTHER: That's not fair, Dr. Bettelheim.

DR. B.: Well, did I ever say I was going to be fair? Everybody knows I'm not fair.[1]

MOTHER: Well, it's just that I want her to grow up to be——

DR. B.: —a rebel! I know because you told us so. And you already want her to rebel against the scheme of values of your neighbors. So, on the one hand you select middle-class neighbors and expose your child to their influence, and on the other hand you want her to fight it. But that's unfair to children. I mean, you can say that you want your child to be a rebel. That's a perfectly legitimate desire in terms of your own needs. But what you do with your child seems to me quite conducive to making a clothes-horse out of her; which would be quite a healthy reaction to your desire to make her a rebel. Because children don't like to be forced into a pattern any more than we do.

MOTHER: But . . . the neighbors aren't that important.

DR. B: But it's you who have exposed her to them. It wasn't the child's own free will to live here. You and your husband haven't given up the advantages of going

1. A brief comment here. Basically what most mothers want is to be helped to be fair with their children. But in helping them to achieve this, many conflicts between parent and child have to be investigated, and while they are still unresolved what may seem fairness to the child may seem like gross unfairness to the mother, or the other way around. So my saying I had no intention of being fair meant (and was usually so understood): I am not interested in being fair to any one party to the conflict. I am intent on solving the conflict, even if it requires being temporarily unfair to one or the other party to it.

to this university to protect your child from the pernicious influence of these middle-class neighbors. [*Sounds of laughter from the group*] Well, nothing wrong with laughing. Much better than crying, believe me. We all need more laughing. But to get back, I'm still talking about how you tear your child apart, and I think it's important that we talk about it. I don't blame you for not having seen it, but my task is to show you the quandaries into which you throw your child. Do you see what I mean?

Your child is still a very inadequately developed individual, still very much subject to the influence you impose on her. She has the natural desire we all have— to be pretty, to be considered good-looking. Certainly, her mother's opinion will be more important than the neighbors', up to a point. You see? But if the neighbors are too unanimous, and if other children she can observe look much more prettily dressed, then you will appear to her not as somebody who's fighting middle-class values (of which she knows nothing at all), but as someone who fights her enjoyment of certain things in life (the admiration or approval of those around her, which is so important to the child). Therefore, just as a child who was extremely deprived orally might become a drunkard, so the child who was extremely deprived (or thought she was) in regard to her clothes, may become a clothes-horse, which is exactly what you're trying to avoid.

But don't you think . . . even given your desire to have a child who will want to reform society . . . that you're better off having someone who is fine, who is good-looking, intelligent, and well-educated and who still is not satisfied with this world because of its inequities, than someone who says, "Nobody thinks I'm good-looking; the whole world is against me; what else can I do but fight it?" Which of the two do you want? And anyway, why don't you enjoy her looking pretty in a dress?

MOTHER: Yes, but still . . . it doesn't seem right to me that a child of three should have a feeling for clothes, or how she looks.

DR. B.: Oh? When does the child have a right to have a feeling for clothes?

SECOND MOTHER: My child started when she was just a year old; she wanted to wear dresses. And sure, it makes a lot more work for me but I get an awful lot of enjoyment out of seeing her look cute.

THIRD MOTHER: Oh, my little girl used to preen when she was just a tiny thing.

DR. B.: Well, I think we understand one another. I think the issue goes much deeper than that. I think your child will resent it if you try to form her into anything. Because your distrust of your child is what worries me. Your feeling that "I have to form you or you won't come out right" is what worries me more than anything. [*Turning*] Why do you shake your head?

THIRD MOTHER: My mother did that to me! "I have to form you . . . or else."

SECOND MOTHER: Well, my mother brought me up thinking that clothes aren't important, and they are. Not the be-all and end-all of existence, but up to a point.

DR. B.: Sure they are. Well . . . have we answered your question? And as you see, I couldn't answer with a "Yes" or "No."

MOTHER: I guess I just never realized how deep down it went.

DR. B.: Because really what you do, and your neighbor to your right has expressed it, you give the child the feeling that "I don't trust you in the normal course of events to grow up to be the best human being I can think of. I have to form you or else." And that comes out of your deep sense of resentment—the one that pushed you around so hard that you landed here at the University of Chicago!

4

Free Elections

FATHER: I have a question. We have two sons, one twenty-eight months and a baby just four months old. And the question has come up of when should the oldest stop having his bottle. I was wondering about that. At night he does ask for his bottle and we've been giving him the excuse that he might wet his bed at night, that perhaps he ought to do without it. Of course, if he absolutely insists, he gets his bottle. But if he doesn't insist . . . no bottle.

DR. B.: Well, that raises the problem I tried to discuss last time—namely, what kind of a child you want to have. You've given me a question and expect me to give you an answer, which would neither be the right answer nor the wrong one, as if there were such a thing. It all depends on what kind of child you want to have.

FATHER: Well, what choices do I have? Apparently I do have a choice.

DR. B.: It's not *one* choice, my friend. Like everything in life, parenthood is a continuous series of choices, and it seems to me that one of the major difficulties in child rearing nowadays is this belief in the experts. It's given people the idea that they can get away from making choices and avoid responsibility for what they do choose. In my opinion that's a totally erroneous notion. You speak about nursing and weaning from the bottle. But as you know, there are cultures where nursing in our sense stops at anywhere from four to six months, and there are other cultures where the child is nursed up to four years and even longer. So you see, if children grow up to adulthood in both cultures and fulfill whatever the culture asks of them, both are equally possible.

FATHER: Well, as far as the conventions of society are concerned, I'm not really interested in that. Whether the baby wants his bottle for six years, it's all right with me. But the question is, is it harmful to take it away?

DR. B.: Now, look. What you say is a contradiction. You say that as far as you're concerned he can have it till he's six. On the other hand you ask if it's harmful to take it away. These two questions you throw at me together, but they imply a contradiction . . . and you haven't told me yet what kind of a child you want to have.

FATHER: Oh, we're very happy with him as he is. He's a sweet-natured boy and he minds very well. When his brother came along he showed the normal amount of jealousy, and . . .

DR. B.: All right. May I interrupt? To begin with— do you want him to believe that his father is a liar, or a man who speaks the truth?

FATHER: Well, you've decided the question for me.

DR. B.: That's right. Now, is it really true that a bottle in the evening, by itself, is what makes the child wet his bed at night?

FATHER: No, of course not.

DR. B.: But you've told him that.

FATHER: That's right.

DR. B.: That's my answer.

FATHER: Well, he accepts it.

DR. B.: Ah! I haven't asked you if he accepts it. I've asked you whether, in the eyes of your child, you can justify it. After all, he'll want to please you, because by and large you're a good parent and you mean well. So he accepts what you say. But sooner or later he'll find out that you've told him an untruth. Now, how are you going to justify it to him? That's my question. You're an intelligent and well-meaning father; I'm assuming you had some purpose in telling him this lie. Wouldn't it be better to analyze your purpose now, and get it clear?

FATHER: I don't understand what you mean.

DR. B.: Well, look. What you're trying to tell me and the group is that you didn't think or had no purpose in telling him such a thing. But it isn't true. You did have a purpose.

FATHER: Well, of course. We had to have an excuse, some intelligent reason to use, in order to go on with our thinking.

DR. B.: But what was your purpose?

FATHER: To stop the bottle in the evening at bedtime.

DR. B.: Yes. But why did you want to stop the bottle at bedtime?

FATHER: One less bottle to wash . . .

DR. B.: I don't believe it! Now you make yourself out worse than you are. You see, this doesn't go with me. A parent who comes to such a meeting and asks such a question is not a parent who is willing to sacrifice the well-being of his child in order to wash a bottle less. Don't make yourself out worse than you are. You're not that bad.

FATHER: Well, is the bottle that important?

DR. B.: If it's unimportant you wouldn't make an issue of it. Since you make it an issue, it must be an important one to you. I didn't make it an issue.

FATHER: Yes, I know. When you break a child of the bottle, it depends on how you break him. It can be a dangerous thing.

DR. B.: But my point is, why do you want to break him of the bottle? That's still my question.

FATHER: Well, I really ought to have my wife here. She might be able to give you an intelligent answer. Maybe it's just time to stop. I don't know . . .

DR. B.: Why? What do you mean, time to stop?

FATHER: Well, there's no universal law . . .

DR. B.: All right. Then why do you say, time to stop. Do you mean, "I as a parent have decided that it's time to stop?"

FATHER: That's probably the answer.

DR. B.: Yes, but I'd like to know why you decided that.

FATHER: Well, we didn't ourselves. It just seems to be a trend.

DR. B.: Whose trend?

FATHER: My wife's trend, more or less.

DR. B.: Well, then, I'm sorry. I cannot argue because your wife isn't here. I can only help you. If your wife were here I'd be happy to discuss it with her. But don't now go home and push it all off on her. Because if you were now to talk things over with her you wouldn't really be able to explain what we were up to in this discussion. Suddenly you wish to stop, which is fine with me. But don't think you've accomplished anything. It's only made you uncomfortable and hasn't solved any problems.

FATHER: Well, why not let the child suck his bottle till he's twelve? There's no objection to that, certainly. Is there?

DR. B.: Is there?

FATHER: I wouldn't think so.

DR. B.: All right. Then at what point do you think he would stop?

FATHER: Well, maybe when his younger brother has given up the bottle.

DR. B.: Or at the age of twelve years? Why would he stop at any time?

FATHER: Well, he's such a big boy now, it's time he did stop.

FATHER: What do you mean, time to stop? There are other babies around who have bottles at his age.

FATHER: Well, yes. But by a certain age we like to think they've grown up and progressed.

DR. B.: But his contemporaries still have it.

SECOND FATHER: Well, he'll find out by a certain age that nobody else drinks from the bottle, and . . .

DR. B.: Just a moment. Do you do what everybody else does all the time?

SECOND FATHER: Well, we generally follow . . .

DR. B.: Do you do what everybody else does?

SECOND FATHER: Yes, but not all the time.

DR. B.: All right. When do you do what everybody else does, and when don't you? You see . . . you make your children out to be freaks who have no feelings like everybody else. But your children are motivated by exactly the same kind of feelings that motivate you.

MOTHER: It's true that what other children do is important! I remember I was a very poor eater and my mother fed me long after other children weren't being fed. But once another child said, "Oh, your mother still feeds you," and immediately I felt I must be doing something wrong, I'm a baby. And it made me very ashamed of the fact that my mother still fed me.

DR. B.: So why did you stop having your mother feed you?

MOTHER: Because I was feeling ashamed.

DR. B.: That's right! And what kind of feeling is that, to be ashamed?

MOTHER: Oh, it's a very bad feeling.

DR. B.: Yes, it's an unpleasant feeling. So why did you give it up?

MOTHER: Well, because it was much more unpleasant to be ridiculed than to feed myself.

DR. B.: Because suddenly, for one reason or another—and for each individual it's different—it was no longer pleasant. And that's my answer! A child stops sucking the bottle when the bottle is no longer pleasant, and that's when you give something up: when you're ready to give it up, or when the doctor tells you to or you'll have a heart attack.

MOTHER: But I can understand how he feels, because everybody comes around and says, "Your daughter isn't toilet trained yet!" and they think that's terrible, though I haven't listened to them and she still isn't trained. So I know what he means. People think it's more or less terrible that a child by a certain age hasn't stopped doing the babyish thing.

DR. B.: Well, that's what I mean when I say that you have to decide: for what or for whom do I educate my child. Didn't I start out with that?

FATHER: Yes, you did start that way.

DR. B.: Because that is the issue. Do you educate your child for the neighbors? Then you do one thing. If you educate your child to get excellent grades in school even at the cost of his happiness, that's another thing. Then you have to proceed differently. If you want your child to hate you then you proceed in one way, and if you want your child to love you then you proceed in another. There is no one way. That's why I couldn't answer your question; because I don't know. I don't know what's the right time to withdraw the bottle, or to break the child from the bottle, or whatever you call it. It all depends on how you want to raise your child.

FATHER: Can it be harmful, though, to break the child of the bottle sooner than he's ready to give it up?

DR. B.: Harmful in what respect?

FATHER: I don't know. I suppose from the mental point of view.

DR. B.: What is a mental point of view?

FATHER: Well, it might leave him with some feeling of insecurity, perhaps.

DR. B.: Look, if you take the bottle away what's the only kind of feeling it can leave him with?

FATHER: With frustration, perhaps, if he needs his bottle badly.

DR. B.: Perhaps . . . I don't know. Because the feeling of frustration doesn't depend on what happens just to bottles alone. You know that when you're frustrated there are many more factors involved than one single issue. But you've only presented one issue to me, and I haven't seen the child. I know nothing about him. How would I know what's wrong or right for the child? I can't discuss a child I've never seen or haven't studied. Do you see what I mean? I can only teach you a way of thinking so that you who know the child, who are very close to the child, who are very concerned about the child, can be better informed.

A while ago you were a little annoyed because I wouldn't tell you "Yes" or "No." Well, this annoyance I have to accept because only you have the answer. Up to now you have acted without much thinking. All I can show you is the danger of doing such things without thinking them through. But now you'll have to think through what you really want to achieve and how you want to achieve it.

What you must reckon with is that every step you take will have its consequences. If you indulge your child and let him have the bottle till he's twelve, that will have consequences. [*Turning to mother*] That your mother spoon-fed you up to a certain age had consequences. I don't think your mother thought much about the consquences, but it had consequences. On the other hand, if your mother had never spoon-fed you, it too, would have had consequences. You know? Consequences are different in nature.

THIRD FATHER: Well, ye gods, every time you discipline your child or do something—either break him of a bottle, or toilet train him, or don't toilet train him— there's the possibility that sixty years later your child is going to hate you for it.

DR. B.: Correct. Very much so.

THIRD FATHER: But ... what the hell ... I can't go through life worrying about whether one or the other of my kids is going to feel pushed around at every experience. After all, the total sum of their experiences is good.

DR. B.: Who decides that?

THIRD FATHER: The children decide it.

DR. B.: Exactly!

THIRD FATHER: The kids are happy. They seem to be. I don't know, but they seem to be. And if, later on, they get mad at me because I switched around their highchairs to make room for the baby, I can't help it.

DR. B.: Correct. You can't help it if the child resents certain of your actions. What counts is, that you should be able, at any one moment, to reasonably justify your actions to the child. A child could resent it that you send him to school. But if the child asks you later on, "Why did you send me to school? I didn't want to go to school,"—don't you think you'll be able to make a reasonable case for why you sent him to school?

THIRD FATHER: Of course.

DR. B.: Don't you think that even the child himself, after he's reached the age of reason, will be able to explain your behavior to himself without even having to ask you?

THIRD FATHER: That's quite possible.

DR. B.: All right. Now, it seems to me that this type of action every parent has to take. These are necessary actions. The question is, in this particular case, is it necessary to break the child from the bottle at this point? And if so, why is it done? And there our friend hasn't given me any help. Therefore I cannot help him. You see, he hasn't told me the whole truth. Because not washing one more bottle is not the true reason, I'm sorry to say.

FATHER: I wish I could give you an intelligent answer. I can't.

DR. B.: But I don't want an intelligent one. I want a true answer. [*To mother*] What was your hesitation about not pushing your child into toilet training?

THIRD FATHER: Because society is against it?

DR. B.: Not society! Who is this society? That's another one of the bugaboos we scare ourselves with.

101

Society never influences you; I never met Mr. or Mrs. Society. Whom *do* you meet?

THIRD FATHER: Friends . . .

DR. B.: Friends! All right, who else?

THIRD FATHER: The grandparents.

DR. B.: The grandparents! That's much closer. So when you speak of society, you always have someone specific in mind. And it's the same with the children. There are no general children. Some children are toilet trained at one year, or taken off the bottle at a year, and don't show some of these features you describe, or a few others I could mention. Some children develop well who were pushed too early into what we call pseudo-maturity. Why then do these notions develop about harmful effects? The answer is that human beings are quite different. Therefore it's no good to look at another child, the child of another mother, who says that her Johnny was trained at a year, and you look at Johnny and see he's a wonderful kid—you still have to decide whether you want your child to be like this Johnny, no matter what price your kid has to pay for it, or whether no matter what, you want to do the right thing by your own child. After all, we can't gauge our child's innate abilities for growth, and maturation, and speed of development. We have no yardstick to measure that yet. What's still the only yardstick we can apply?

THIRD FATHER: The child itself.

DR. B.: That's right. The child itself. So my question remains: why do you think it's necessary to break the child of the bottle? That's what I'd still like to know.

FATHER: There's nothing necessary about it. It's just easier on our icebox. That's the truth.

DR. B.: Now, look. I have children of my own, and I know that the number of bottles is really such a small thing that I don't understand you. As a matter of fact, with the sanitation code of this city, you don't even have to sterilize after six months or a year; so it's no more work than washing a glass.

FATHER: Did you break your children of the bottle?

DR. B.: No.

FATHER: You never did that?

DR. B.: Never.

FATHER: When did they give them up?

DR. B.: When they said so.

FATHER: Oh . . . well, how old were they?

DR. B.: One of them discarded the night bottle when she was three and a half.

FATHER: And she didn't take one during the day?

DR. B.: No. That she stopped when she was two and a half.

FATHER: What did she do? Did she tell you she didn't want her bottle one day?

DR. B.: Yes.

FATHER: She just said, "No more bottle"?

DR. B.: That's right.

FATHER: I think they're very intelligent . . .

DR. B.: No! I think any child will do that. That's my point. Any child will do that, and that's why I was glad when this lady gave her example. At one moment she decided that to be spoon-fed was unpleasant, and then and there she gave it up. Wasn't that how it happened? And even with some resistance by your mother?

MOTHER: Yes, she thought I would starve to death.

DR. B.: That's right, you gave it up, despite your mother's resistance. You see, this was a mother who tried to force a bottle, so to speak. But the kid wouldn't take it, because it was no longer pleasant. That's when we all give things up. So the question is—since we all know this—why do you want to force your child to give it up before such a time?

FATHER: Well, I agree with you 100 per cent on that.

DR. B.: No, no, I don't want agreement. I want you to tell me.

FATHER: The only problem is our friends. The only problem is my mother. She compares our baby with her other grandchild, and so forth. And if that's the answer you want, that's the answer.

DR. B.: That's right. Who does it better? Who does it faster?

FATHER: Well, *can* you break a child from the bottle?

DR. B.: Of course you can. Human beings are extremely malleable.

FATHER: Oh, I know you can, if you let them cry. The point is, can you break them without letting them cry too much?

DR. B.: Now, look. The crying . . . that doesn't—excuse me—mean a damned thing to me for the following reasons: because people are born with differing amounts of strength, and differing amounts of strength of resistance. That one child wails for the bottle and so forces you to continue the bottle where the other child doesn't, means only one thing to me—that the one child has more power to fight back. But it by no means signifies that the other child has less desire for the bottle. Do you follow?

All you're saying is that the first one can kick more, and then you jump to the conclusion that he wants the bottle more, which is a non sequitur. You just cannot measure a person's desire for a thing by the fuss he puts up at not getting it. There are individuals who want a thing very much but will never ask for it. Does that really mean that they don't want it? It's just that they're the sort of persons who will swallow their frustration, or their anger, or their unhappiness, and won't ask. Other people want something not very badly. But even if they want it only a little, they make a terrible fuss. Does that really mean that they want a thing more than the one who doesn't yell? Do you see the error in such thinking?

FATHER: Yes.

DR. B.: All right. As I said before, I can only teach you a way of thinking. That's why I can never tell you what to do with your child. Because to go back—if you, in your own mind, and your wife, too, are going to feel badly about his backwardness compared to your brother's child, if you really feel strongly about it, then in the last analysis it might be better to break him of the bottle sooner. If you were now to give the bottle back to your child, though each time he grabs for it you feel, "Ugh, why aren't you as far ahead as my brother's son . . ."

FATHER: Oh, it's not really that bad.

DR. B.: Well, of course not. But I exaggerate to make a point, to show that nothing is gained by giving him a bottle that way. It's very easy for me to say, "Give him his bottle," but that might be the totally wrong thing for you to do. Because if you do it with misgivings then it's better not to give it at all.

SECOND MOTHER: Can I say something here? It seems to me that during the last ten or twelve years an awful lot of stress has been put on toilet training and the bottle. My own daughter is twelve now; she's older. But it wasn't such a bugaboo when my children were little. The threat of all this impending doom didn't hang over our heads that strongly. Has it really been proven that it's so important, ultimately? *I* took the bottle away from my children . . .

DR. B.: Look, I didn't start this discussion on the bottle because I consider it a vital issue. For me any issue is a good one to teach you a way of thinking.

SECOND MOTHER: But it must be important! All these younger people are so impressed with it . . .

DR. B.: Well, that brings us back to an old problem I have with so many groups of parents. They tell me, "I mustn't give in to my child; he has to learn to accept frustrations now, because ten years later, or thirty years later, he might not stand up in competition, or what not." And the same parents are utterly convinced that within three years we will all be wiped out by atomic bombs. But these two together just don't make sense.

I'm as afraid of the bomb and a war with Russia as the next guy. Therefore, since I'm not at all convinced that my children will survive the next decade or so, I want them to have as much fun while they're alive as I can give them. And it's not a question of doom tomorrow so let's make hay. It's just my feeling that if they like it better, if it's more fun and harms nobody, why shouldn't I? Life is difficult enough. Why should I withdraw a pleasure I can very well give them? That, it seems to me, is the issue at stake.

FATHER: Well, then you're making the point that the bottle is a pleasure?

DR. B.: Oh, most certainly! Otherwise the child wouldn't cry for it.

FATHER: Well, once again, how about the individual child from whom you take it away because he also drinks out of a glass. So you're denying him pleasure without meaning to.

DR. B.: Look. Who decides what's pleasure? You or the child?

FATHER: The child.

DR. B.: All right. If you put a glass here and a bottle there, and the child takes the glass and neglects the bottle, doesn't that settle the issue? And if the child takes the bottle and neglects the glass, doesn't that settle the issue? So where's the problem? I don't see it.

FATHER: Well, sometimes there's reason to consider what the neighbors think. Anyway ... I mean ... living in an area where most babies give up the bottle by three, and your baby's still asking for it at five, you do look at his development somewhat in the light of how other children develop. Wouldn't you begin to wonder, then, if something isn't wrong?

DR. B.: Look, all my life I've worked with very disturbed children, which naturally increases a parent's anxiety about his own child. Well, strangely enough, I haven't been afraid for my children. I certainly never gave a hoot about the bottle. I will not say that I didn't suggest to my child that she should go to the toilet, that she's a big girl and why doesn't she go to the toilet. So she gave me a big laugh and said "in a year" she would do it. "Good for you," I said, "If you say a year . . ." A year didn't mean anything to her, you know; it was just an answer.

But of course it would have been foolish if I had never told her that I wanted her to go to the toilet. How else would she get the idea? Of cousre you have to suggest it. And when the child goes for the first time, you make a big to-do about it, and you're very happy, because otherwise how would she learn?

FATHER: Well, isn't that toilet training, Dr. Bettelheim?

DR. B.: Of course it's toilet training! Did I ever say you shouldn't toilet train your child?

FATHER: No-o-o.

DR. B.: Did I ever tell you that you shouldn't present the glass to your child? And if the child says, "I want to drink out of a glass," do you say, "Oh, no, my child, you must indulge yourself. Go back to the bottle." Now, that would be foolish. Then you'd have a misfit. But to my knowledge, and with reasonable people, I haven't encountered such foolishness. That just doesn't happen.

FATHER: Well, maybe one can break a child of the bottle by . . . well, by praising him so highly for drinking from a glass. Would you find fault with that?

DR. B.: No. Only I would ask, why do you want to praise your child so highly? That is, why do you want to push your child away from the bottle?

FATHER: Well, why do you want him to go to the toilet? You just gave an example. I don't know. Evidently there was a time with your children when you wanted to break them, or toilet train them, and you

107

suggested that they ought to go and they went. You did all that, just like a good parent. What were your reasons? What are any parent's reasons?

DR. B.: That you enjoy it when your child reaches a higher level of maturity. That's natural. Any parent enjoys it, and this enjoyment you might as well show to your child. But that wasn't what you asked me. If you'd asked me, "What shall I do when my child, out of his own volition, gives up the bottle?" my answer would have been different. But you ask me, "When should my child stop having his bottle?" which is entirely different than if the child does it on his own.

And I'll tell you quite frankly: if you didn't drink out of glasses, no child would spontaneously develop the desire to drink out of a glass. If you didn't go to the toilet, and the child didn't have any notion that you do, no child would ever develop such a notion. Because there are many cultures where the people do not drink out of glasses but out of bowls, and then the training is that they learn to drink out of bowls. Because good, sound learning is based on the fact that the child who has a good relationship to his parents will imitate them. But he will imitate his parents best if you don't force him to do so, when he's good and ready for it, and not before.

III

Are They So Different?

1

A Chance to Be Heard

MOTHER: I have something different on my mind. John's had a hard time recently because the older kids have been pushing him around at nursery school. I haven't been there consistently, but when I have, it's been one particular child who's a leader and has one or two followers. They start in with, "Hello, dopey," or "Shut up," or they hit him.

DR. B.: And what do the teachers say?

MOTHER: They don't seem to do anything that I've noticed.

DR. B.: Why?

MOTHER: Well, I'm going to talk to them.

DR. B.: Yes, I would do that.

MOTHER: It's gotten to the point where every day he comes home and says, "Stevie hit me today," or "Stevie didn't hit me," or "Stevie did such and such."

DR. B.: Still, you realize you're only getting one side of the story.

MOTHER: I know, and I don't understand what's cooking.

DR. B.: That's right. I think you have to talk with the teacher.

MOTHER: Well, in the meantime what can I do to explain this hitting business he keeps questioning me about?

DR. B.: Does he like to go to nursery school every morning?

MOTHER: It's in the afternoon, and he does like it.

DR. B.: Does he really like to go?

MOTHER: Yes.

DR. B.: Very much?

MOTHER: Well, most of the time. Occasionally not, but most of the time very much.

DR. B.: Then, as long as he likes to go I wouldn't worry too much.

MOTHER: Okay.

DR. B.: You see what I mean? If it were too bad, he wouldn't like to go. But I still think you should find out what goes on.

MOTHER: Well, I've wondered, too. But right now he doesn't know if he should hit back or not, and I've taken the tack that it would probably be better if he just kept away from Stevie, or anybody who bothers him.

DR. B.: Well, that's a bad tack.

MOTHER: It is?

DR. B.: Yes.

MOTHER: All right. Now what should I . . . that's the reason . . . that's why I'm asking you. Because I haven't felt satisfied with my own answers.

DR. B.: Well, why do you think I call it a bad tack?

MOTHER: Well, I don't want to tell him, "Yes," he can hit back.

DR. B.: What's wrong with this? Maybe you did say the right thing to your son, but what's wrong with your statement as we've heard it?

MOTHER: Okay, what's wrong? That's what I want to know. I'm dissatisfied. Because he keeps questioning me, and it obviously doesn't satisfy him.

DR. B.: That's exactly the point!

MOTHER: It isn't any solution . . . to just tell him to stay away.

DR. B.: It's an answer to a question he didn't ask.

MOTHER: Oh!

DR. B.: No, I don't think you see it yet, but it's very

112

important. Let's go over it again, very carefully, and see if somebody can help us find out.

MOTHER: Maybe I ought to tell you more about our conversations.

DR. B.: That's a good idea.

MOTHER: Well, it's the same conversation we've had every day now for a couple of weeks. He'll start off with, "Stevie hit me today." And I say, "That's too bad. I'm sorry he hit you," and then I hope he'll drop the subject. But he says, "Nobody came to help me out." And I say, "Well, did you need help?" And he says, "Oh, yes." And I say, "Well, what did you do?" And he says, "I didn't do anything." And I say, "Well, if you need help, call a teacher," and he says, "I want to hit Stevie back. Should I hit Stevie back? Is that all right?" And I say, "It's probably better to keep away from him if he's going to hit. It's not nice of him to hit, but I'd rather that you didn't hit." And . . .

DR. B.: May I interrupt for a moment? If a child says "I want to jump out the window," would you say, "It's probably a bad idea"?

MOTHER: Yes . . . that's . . . yes, I see. You say "No."

DR. B.: The Bible says, "Say yes, yes, or no, no." The Bible doesn't say to tell him, "Probably."

MOTHER: That's why I feel the dissatisfaction.

DR. B.: That's only the first step in this thing. We haven't even begun to discuss the real matter. The child wants a piece of information from a parent who supposedly knows better than he does. If a parent knows only "Probably," what is the poor child going to know?

MOTHER: Yes, I see.

DR. B.: All right. Now . . . if he asks you whether it's going to rain tomorrow or whether the sun will shine, there you have no choice. Why don't you have any choice?

MOTHER: Because you don't know.

DR. B.: That's only part of it.

MOTHER: You have no control over it.

DR. B.: You have no control over it! That's the answer. The unknowns, you know; and there are many different types of unknowns. After all, it's unknown if you'll be alive tomorrow, but you still say, "I will feed you tomorrow." But why, when you really don't know if you'll actually be able to? Because everything we say contains some probability. And, as you know, when you mean that, you don't say, "Probably." You just take it for granted. So, unless you have a doubt in your mind, why do you say, "Probably?"

MOTHER: The reason for the "Probably" is that I feel very badly about it. That's the real reason. In most instances I can say "Yes" or "No," but in this case . . .

DR. B.: All right. So your boy comes home and reasons, "Those kids at nursery school made me feel bad. Now I'll come home and make mommy feel bad about me, because then her heart goes out to me."

MOTHER: No, I feel bad because I've seen him with watery eyes.

DR. B.: Sure, sure. Many eyes have watered because it makes people feel badly to see it. Look, can we start all over? Let's look at the rest of the story. Just give us the essence of it.

MOTHER: The essence is, uh . . .

DR. B.: All right, may I tell the story? And if I don't tell it right, you correct me.

MOTHER: Okay.

DR. B.: But don't hesitate to interrupt me. Now, if we bring the story down to its essence we'll understand why the "Probably" is a bad idea. The child is hit—as far as we know without reason or provocation. The child feels badly about it. He comes home and says, "I'm unhappy because I was hit."

MOTHER: No, he reports either "Stevie hit me" or "He didn't hit me."

DR. B.: Hm? Well, today he reports, "Stevie hit me."

The mother says, "Did you ask for help?" "There was nobody to help me," the boy says. "I want to hit back; shall I?" The mother says, "That's not a very good idea." Is that it?

MOTHER: Yes.

DR. B.: Is there any more to it?

MOTHER: I told him I don't want him to hit. That I think it's a bad thing to hit.

DR. B.: Yes, it's a bad thing to hit. Do you all understand the story? Now, what's wrong with this story? What should the mother have done? [*Turning*] Do you have an idea?

SECOND MOTHER: No, I have the same problem.

DR. B.: Oh, that's why you looked so understanding.

SECOND MOTHER: Well, the child has to defend himself, doesn't he?

DR. B.: If I were confronted with Joe Louis, even at his most dilapidated, I wouldn't defend myself, either. I'd run.

THIRD MOTHER: If the mother doesn't feel strongly enough, well, the mother's uncertain. She doesn't quite know what she wants the child to do.

MOTHER: No, I know what I want.

FOURTH MOTHER: You can comfort the child for having been hit and not say anything about what the child should do.

DR. B.: Well, I don't know. Maybe you've done what I'm going to suggest now, but I'll take over now, to make sure we all get it. I've spent time on this one because I think it's another central issue. And it's an issue, not because of this particular case, but because of the particular mistake I believe I detect. One of you brought it to the fore ... that the mother doesn't know what she wants the child to do. Can you take it from there?

MOTHER: In a way that's right and in another way it's wrong. I know what I'd like him to do, how I'd like him to handle it. But I don't know how I can help him do it.

DR. B.: That's exactly what's wrong.

MOTHER: That I want him to know?

DR. B.: That you have strong feelings about the way you want him to handle it. That you know what your feelings are, but not his.

MOTHER: Oh, I see.

DR. B.: The issue is to *ask* him. Not, "That's a good idea, that's a bad idea," or you wouldn't like him to do that. The question is, "What did you feel like doing?"

MOTHER: Well, I think . . . gosh . . . it seems . . .

DR. B.: You impose your choices on him whatever you do—whether you say, "Hit" or "Don't hit," or "Call the teacher." You say, by implication, "I'm convinced you can't handle the situation on your own." He already knows that, or feels it, and you hit right back into it. Therefore it's immaterial whether you say, "Hit back," or "Defend yourself," or "Run away." You hand him your opinion, without asking him for his.

MOTHER: Oh, you mean . . .

DR. B.: "Stevie hit you. What did you feel like doing, and what did you actually do?"

MOTHER: Oh, well the reason I didn't think of that, the simplest thing, is because he said, "Is it all right to hit back?" So I assumed that that's what he felt like doing. But it might not have been . . .

DR. B.: He may just have been testing you out. He may have wanted to get the go-ahead sign from you, your telling him that he has a right to act in accordance with his own feelings instead of with yours.

MOTHER: That's right. Yes . . .

SECOND MOTHER: But doesn't civilization impose a pattern on you about things like this?

THIRD MOTHER: I was going to say the opposite. Don't children instinctively do at any moment what they feel like doing?

MOTHER: No, because John wouldn't necessarily

want to hit back right away. He might, but it's not necessarily what he'd want.

DR. B.: Well, now. Not only do I have to deal with a three-and-a-half-year-old child but with instincts and civilization, too.

MOTHER: Well, what should you do after you've asked him that question? Say his instinct was that he wanted to hit back. Should you let him, then, if that's what he wanted to do at the moment?

DR. B.: Not necessarily. But then at least I'd have been clear where he stands and where I stand, and then I'd know what to say, I think. I'd say to him, "Well, that's okay. Lots of times we want to hit back. Lots of times I want to, myself," and then we'd talk about it; what's good about it and what's bad.

SECOND MOTHER: You still say nothing, then, about what he should do?

MOTHER: You keep away from him?

DR. B.: Did I ever say that?

MOTHER: No, you say you've got to ask him what he wants to do. But what do you do from then on? After he ...

DR. B.: That depends on his answer.

SECOND MOTHER: Oh.

MOTHER: Well, so he says he wants to hit back. Then what would you say? "Go right ahead?"

DR. B.: Well, I'd say, "If that's what you wanted, why didn't you do it?"

MOTHER: Oh.

SECOND MOTHER: What if he says he's afraid to?

DR. B.: Ahh ... Now then, at least we know the situation. That this child would like to hit back but is afraid to. Now is when civilization and our instincts come in, and then the mother has to decide what she wants to do about it.

MOTHER: Well, what do you do about it?

DR. B.: The first thing you can do is to give him the conviction that you respect his opinion and are inter-

117

ested in it. Very often we cannot exactly agree with the child, but we can at least give him the privilege of hearing him out first on his own opinion before we impose our opinion on him.

MOTHER: You mean he wants to be treated as a human being and not as a baby.

DR. B.: *That's right!* He wants to be treated like a human being, particularly when he's in distress. And he wants to hear from his mother that his own feelings count more with his mother than what civilization says.

MOTHER: Or even more than what happened.

DR. B.: Or what the mother's particular attitude is about pacifism and war.

SECOND MOTHER: Well, what's wrong with wanting a peace-loving child?

DR. B.: Nothing. That's what guided this mother.

MOTHER: Yes, I agree with you. I don't want an aggressive son. I don't want him to hit.

DR. B.: That's right, and he knew it all along. So the real issue . . . what really stymies your child is the contradiction between his own aggressive tendencies and your desire to have a nonaggressive child.

MOTHER: Yes, I told him that I didn't want him to hit.

DR. B.: Well, let's see now . . . so who created the difficulty at nursery school in the first place?

MOTHER: Now, look. That I don't believe.

DR. B.: All right. Let's take it slowly. You want to bring your child up in a particular way. Now, while I agree that it's a desirable pattern, it's by no means a prevailing pattern. But then you also want to put the burden of that choice on the child, and that you cannot do. You bring him into a difficult situation and then you want to put the burden on him. That's too much for a three-year-old to carry.

MOTHER: I agree. Because it wouldn't necessarily have to be Stevie; it could be anybody.

DR. B.: That's right. The difficulty, and his frustration, don't come from the push or the slap he got from Stevie. Yes?

MOTHER: I agree. Because Stevie doesn't hit hard.

DR. B.: That's right. It's the issue that stymies him. He cannot ask the teacher because the teacher might very well tell him to hit back, which would only increase his conflict between his inner desire, the teacher, and you.

MOTHER: Another thing. I might as well tell you something that I realized half way through this business. By telling him to keep away from Stevie I had ... I realized somewhere that ... oh, I know when! I saw John *not* keeping away from Stevie, but trying to play with Stevie and this other little boy and managing to play with him very happily one day. And I suddenly realized that by telling him to avoid a difficult situation I was also keeping him from good times.

DR. B.: That's right! And one could finally come to avoid all social intercourse because any intercourse involves conflict and the danger of being hurt.

MOTHER: Yes. This has come up here in several other instances in the past, all of them around the hitting business ...

DR. B.: That's right! This telling him to avoid the issue—well, remember we had this some time ago? The issue came up of what should the mother tell the kid who comes home and says. "I was hit in the back yard by one of the other children"? And I told you it was up to the child. "Look, my kid. These other children, I think they're nasty to hit, but it's up to you. If you don't want to be hit, stay here. I'll be happy to have you with me. But if you want to play with these children, you'll have to take your chances of being hit." And the kid then knows what's right for him; some days he stays in, other days he turns and goes out again.

MOTHER: Yes, John will keep going to nursery school.

DR. B.: That's right. That's why I asked first, "Does he like to go to nursery school?"

MOTHER: That's right.

DR. B.: The point is that it's hard to instill our own values in a child when they contradict the values of the community or when the pattern of how we want our child to behave is not in line with the pattern of the majority, or a sizable minority, of the other children.

MOTHER: It's a big problem.

DR. B.: Yes, but it's unavoidable. I think if you want to educate your child decently, you sometimes have to educate him out of line with the mores of the majority. That's unavoidable. But then, at least you must give him a chance to be heard. And see to it that he does it only if he wants to do it.

MOTHER: And can take some of the responsibility.

DR. B.: That's most important; not that he *can* take the responsibility, but that he *wants* to take it, and on his own. And for him to be able to do that, you must realize that it's you who created the difficulty in the first place—not Stevie, and not your boy. You did it. And after you've made sure that he understands that, then he can take care of the situation on his own, as he thinks best.

MOTHER: Therefore it's unnecessary for me to talk to the teacher.

DR. B.: That I don't know. But it may be that he doesn't want to add to his inner conflict by hearing the teacher say something that's contrary to what your values are.

MOTHER: Today for the first time he did ask me what the teachers felt about hitting.

DR. B.: See? Then we weren't far off.

MOTHER: Yes, its quite possible.

DR. B.: Now, let's go back to civilization.

SECOND MOTHER: I have a question about your last statement. You say that there'd be inner conflict. Wouldn't the child be aware of the mother's attitude anyway—presumably the attitude of the home toward hitting?

DR. B.: Oh, sure. Life is a long series of conflicts. The question is between what or whom is the conflict. Do you see what I mean? No, I guess you don't.

SECOND MOTHER: No, I don't.

DR. B.: Well, suppose then you tell me what you really want to know.

SECOND MOTHER: Well, it seems that in any case there's a conflict between the outer world—in this case it's the family that doesn't wish an aggressive act—and his own desires.

DR. B.: That's right.

SECOND MOTHER: Hence my remark about civilization, to which you objected.

DR. B.: I don't think you should blame it on civilization. It's our own values; it's the conflict within ourselves that gives us the deep troubles. If we're clear within ourselves, we can manage our conflicts with society quite well. But if we want to hit back and also want to avoid all aggression, we're already in a mess; and if society then demands or expects something still different, then we're paralyzed and have to ask others, "What'll I do?" But whatever they suggest is no good, because we can only act successfully after we've solved our own inner conflict.

SECOND MOTHER: But there's a certain pattern that we try to have children conform to; oh, asking for things instead of grabbing, taking turns—the kind of things that babies don't know about until they're taught.

DR. B.: Yes ...

SECOND MOTHER: In any case there's unavoidable conflict.

DR. B.: That's right.

SECOND MOTHER: So I can't see that there's terribly much to gain by asking their opinion. There's a conflict in either case; whether you tell them not to hit or

121

whether you don't, they know you don't want them to, even when you say, "Okay, do whatever you choose."

MOTHER: But I don't know whether he wants to hit, even. I mean, according to what I think right now, he might want to hit back. But then again, he might simply, as Doctor Bettelheim says, be testing me out. How do I know unless I ask him?

DR. B.: Or he's afraid of the other boy, of your opinion, the teacher's opinion, or what not. At the least we can help him to know between what and whom the conflict lies. Still, I don't see what this lady [*the second mother*] is driving at. Something's worrying you. You've got something on your mind and I cannot quite see what you're driving at.

SECOND MOTHER: It just seems that there'd be a conflict no matter what.

DR. B.: That's right.

SECOND MOTHER: Obviously it'll be less if you ask the child, "What do you want to do?" and let him do it. But there will still be the subconscious feeling that you don't particularly approve.

DR. B.: Yes, but that isn't the issue. I'm afraid you fail to see the point I was trying to make. The point is not that you can avoid conflict, but that you can show the child that you understand what's troubling him. That the issue is the conflict and his inability to solve it, and not the being hit. Do you understand the difference?

MOTHER: Yes, I see that.

DR. B.: He comes home, and what he says is, "Stevie hit me and I could have hit back but I didn't." If he could have said, "I wanted to hit back but didn't because you don't want me to, and now I'm unhappy," then he would have understood where his difficulties lay and you could have helped him.

MOTHER: Yes. I'm sure that's it. Because he wouldn't have kept bringing it up weeks in a row. Usually things that he brings up, he brings up for two or three days, we settle it and it's over.[1]

DR. B.: That's right. But in this case he has a tendency to hit back but feels that mommy wouldn't approve of it. And the mother's part, since she's more intelligent and mature, is to understand that, and to help the child where he needs help. He doesn't need help with the fact that Stevie hit him. He needs help with his inner conflicts.

MOTHER: Yes, and I've been giving him moralistic answers.

DR. B.: But those answers only increased his conflict. That's why I said there may be issues where the mother doesn't know what she wants—which is bad. But not as bad as if the mother imposes what she wants without trying to find out what the child wants. After she's done that, and if their wishes still conflict, then she can give him comfort and support where his real struggle is. Do you understand the difference?

SECOND MOTHER: Yes . . . now I understand.

DR. B.: And maybe if he understands what his inner conflict is, he will neither have to hit back nor take it lying down, but find a solution on his three-year-old level which the other kids will be able to accept. Because it'll be a solution that's appropriate not to mother's level or the teacher's, but to his own three-year-old way of understanding the world.

---

1. In the heat of the discussion, I missed this very important clue: that the boy came home again and again reporting such things as "Stevie hit me." If he had been able to accept his mother's attitude, he would have stopped reporting. Since he could not accept it, he came home each time telling her that the methods she wanted him to use did not work, in hopes that his repeated misfortunes would get her to change what she wanted him to do. Fortunately the mother realized this herself when she saw how unusual it was for him to bring the matter up for weeks.

2

Mixed Emotions

MOTHER: I have a little girl two years old who's been playing very nicely for several months with two other children. But lately she's been acting strangely and I can't figure it out. About a week ago she was playing at another child's house and when I took the baby and went after her she'd been crying very hard. Since then, if I take her to visit other children, she always wants to go but then she cries when we get there.

DR. B.: Do you live in the same house as her playmates?

MOTHER: No, but very close.

DR. B.: She wanted to go over but then she didn't want to stay?

MOTHER: Well, she wanted to go and she didn't.

DR. B.: How old is the baby?

MOTHER: Three months.

DR. B.: Well, I'd go very slowly in sending her out.

MOTHER: Alone?

DR. B.: Alone or with you. I'd let her stay home until she really asks. Visitors in your home, okay. But I'd keep her home until she's good and ready to visit other children again.

MOTHER: Well, shall I have the other children come to our house?

DR. B.: If they want to. After all, that's not entirely up to you, is it?

MOTHER: No, but . . .

DR. B.: I don't think a two-year-old needs company every day.

MOTHER: This morning she was very happy until we went out, and after that she was quite disturbed.

DR. B.: Yes. Well, it doesn't pay. Don't forget that by three months the newness of the baby has worn off and his bothersomeness is starting. I wouldn't send her out or suggest it too strongly while the baby still stays home with you.

MOTHER: Well, she seems to like the baby much more than she did at the beginning. She acts as if she genuinely likes him. In fact, today she went up and kissed him for the first time. But she did it all of her own accord when I was paying no attention. I just happened to see it.

DR. B.: Well, as I've tried to explain in the past, the problem of the jealousy of siblings is a good example to show, if you'll excuse me, how dumb we can be about our children. You've read in books that children are jealous of the newcomer. Now, what does jealousy mean?

MOTHER: A definition of it, you mean? Isn't it a displacement? Or what you once owned is no longer yours?

SECOND MOTHER: You don't want to share the same thing.

THIRD MOTHER: You're afraid that the person you love will like somebody else better than you.

DR. B.: Yes and no. What you say is quite typical of the notions we apply nowadays to the problems created by an addition to the family. There's a new baby and the older child should be jealous because he's lost his place. But then the older child runs up and kisses the baby, so obviously this child is not jealous. Wasn't that implied in your statement?

MOTHER: To all appearances, yes.

DR. B.: Now, are the appearances right or are the books right or what's what? After all, this is what

125

enters the mind of any modern mother who has more than one child. The second child is coming and we're all very careful. We know the older child will be jealous, and all these terrible things. We've heard other children say, "Let's send the baby back to the hospital, or to the Lord," or, "Let's give it back to the stork," or what have you. But then the two-year-old runs up and kisses the baby. Well, what's what? What is this jealousy?

SECOND MOTHER: It doesn't have to be expressed by dropping the baby on its head. There are certainly other signs and symptoms.

DR. B.: Yes, you tell me these are symptoms, but you don't tell me what of.

SECOND MOTHER: They're just symptoms of the feeling that the child doesn't feel as secure as it once felt.

MOTHER: Isn't there hostility and hate?

DR. B.: Is there?

MOTHER: Hostility, I should think, would be the end product of the feeling of hate.

DR. B.: Again everything you say is right in a way, and yet it doesn't fit. None of it quite applies, and the reason's very simple. When you talk about jealousy, you talk about the children and never about yourselves. Remember how often we finally arrive at the conclusion, the best way to raise children intelligently is to translate things in your own terms and ask, "How would I feel?" And the issue I'm trying to raise applies not just to jealousy, but to discipline, to aggressions, or what have you. Why don't you translate it in your own terms?

MOTHER: Are you saying, why would you, if you kissed a person you were jealous of, why would you do it? Is that what you're asking?

DR. B.: Yes. What would you feel?

MOTHER: You feel you're missing out on something.

DR. B.: Yes, in a way, but let's be more specific.

SECOND MOTHER: You're learning to conform to what you know is expected of you.

DR. B.: That's *jealousy?* Come on now, talk about yourself. When you're jealous, of whom are you jealous?

THIRD MOTHER: If I'm jealous of someone, I'd try to impress the person.

DR. B.: Were you ever jealous of someone?

THIRD MOTHER: No.

DR. B.: All right. Then you have no knowledge.

THIRD MOTHER: My goodness!

MOTHER: Well, I think when I've been jealous it's been a feeling of, here's something I'm not as good at as that person is.

DR. B.: Exactly!

MOTHER: And they're getting something that I'm not, because of it.

DR. B.: That's right!

MOTHER: So you just sort of give up.

DR. B.: Ah, just a moment. There are some who give up and some who go on from there; so we can't generalize. Now tell me, are you jealous of a person who's of no importance to you?

MOTHER: No.

DR. B.: And the closer you are, the greater your positive feelings are for a person, the more or the less jealous are you going to be?

MOTHER: The more.

DR. B.: So why are you then amazed if your kid goes up and kisses the baby? Jealousy, by definition, is a mixed emotion, isn't it? A combination of love and hate, and not hate alone. The interesting thing is that you know this very well about yourselves. If you hate somebody, you say, "I hate him"; you don't say, "I'm jealous." You would never mix these up in your own case. You know very well the difference between being jealous of someone and hating someone or despising someone. But when it comes to your kids, then jealousy is identical with hate.

Then when you read that children are jealous and you see the child showing love, you're amazed. Wasn't that implied in your initial description and the definitions of jealousy we've heard? Okay, what I wanted to show you is that sometimes you apply different yardsticks for your children than you apply for yourselves. But then you're less apt to be as helpful as if you rightly understood what the child feels when he's troubled by jealousy. Do we all understand one another?

Incidentally, does anyone know Webster's definition of jealousy? Nobody? Well, I know it by heart, because I've had to quote it so often for the same reason it took us some time to figure it out here. Webster says, "Watchful in guarding or keeping." So that's why your little one wants to stick close to home. She wants to keep an eye on the baby so that the baby doesn't get too much of what she wants for herself. As long as you take her to visit her friends, she can still watch what you're doing. But when you leave her there, she can't any more, and so she cries and wants to go home.

Actually, most children aren't jealous of each other, they're jealous of their parents. They want to be sure that the new baby doesn't get too much of mother's love. If they've watched and convinced themselves that it doesn't, then they can kiss it.

Now one last word. If you're jealous of your husband, you won't like it if you know he's visiting somebody and you can't see what he's up to with this other woman. You prefer to stick around and at least know. So does your little girl when she wants to stick around and see what's going on between you and her brother. And when you have really and truly seen that this other woman isn't trying to get your beloved husband away from you, you might even be grateful, become very friendly, and even give her a kiss—as your girl did when she saw that her little brother wasn't taking you entirely away from her.

So you see, it's really very simple as soon as we're convinced that in their situation we'd behave exactly as they do. The actions you can see. But as long as you can't construct from them an analogous situation where you'd behave exactly as they do, you'll have to think back to our discussions again. Because that's all you need to learn, and it's all I can teach you.

3

The Bible, Almost

MOTHER: Doctor Bettelheim, I've wondered about this whole question of aggression in boys. Just recently my three-year-old got fascinated by baseball, and when he did he stopped browbeating his sister.

DR. B.: Or it might be the other way around. How do you know what was cause and what was consequence?

MOTHER: I don't, except that the timing was just right. They both happened at the same time. But what about their aggression? Don't they have to get it out of their systems?

DR. B.: I don't know. But first let's get rid of preconceived notions. They can distort our observations and make us jump to conclusions. You generalize that your children have aggressions, which is very neat; but when you limit it to children, it's an erroneous statement. Why children? Do only children have aggressions?

MOTHER: No, of course not.

DR. B.: All right. Then why say that children have aggressions which they have to work out? Because if you started out with, "People have aggressions," you would immediately ask, "Why should children work it out by shooting, if we disapprove of that in adults?"

MOTHER: You mean, of adults shooting at other adults? I don't understand?

DR. B.: Look, we very often say, "Children need such and such," in this way drawing a line between ourselves and the children, which is always a bad idea.

Now there are certain ways in which children *are* different from adults, and where you say, "Children do such and such" and are perfectly correct. But to say, "Children have aggressions" seems to establish a dichotomy between child and nonchild which is erroneous. That's what I first objected to. As we know, every human being has a great deal of aggression. But if we didn't overlook that, we would never say that children have to work it out by shooting guns, because we know that adults don't work it out that way.

MOTHER: But we do, in periods of war.

DR. B.: Yes, but that isn't a constant. There are periods of peace in between, thank the Lord, and we live in a relatively peaceful society, after all's said and done. I regret that there's fighting going on in Korea, but after all, it's a limited amount of fighting.

Insofar as my knowledge of world history goes, there has never been a time without some fighting going on somewhere, but most of the time it's only been a very small segment of mankind that's been involved. The point is that by and large, in our society, the majority of human beings get along without discharging their aggressions. And we fool ourselves when we establish a dichotomy between children and adults with only children having aggressions.

We have to start out with correct premises if we want to arrive at correct conclusions, and after that we have to find constructive ways of dealing with them. Right now the problem is to find constructive ways of dealing with all types of aggressions, at all ages. If we start out with, "*All* human beings have aggressions," we will not so easily come to the erroneous conclusion that children have to discharge them in gun play.

MOTHER: I want to go over this ... to get it straight in my mind. Very often you read things like "If you've done something to make your child angry, and your child wants to hit you, you should let him; because it's better for the child to hit you and get it over with, his anger at you, than to have him hate you because he can't hit you and then harbors it for a long time."

DR. B.: Very often, you read that?

MOTHER: Well, I've read it a lot.

DR. B.: Where? You must read again and again in the wrong books. It may very well be written, but where? I'm curious.

MOTHER: Well, I think . . . I mean, it's hard to remember where you read these things, but I think I read it in Spock.

DR. B.: He's very good about babies; he's rendered them a great service and I don't wish to disparage him. But I don't think we should ever take a book's statement and follow it. That goes for my own writings, too. Look, do you ever model your life by what the heroine in a novel might do?

MOTHER: But that's not the same thing.

DR. B.: Why not?

MOTHER: Because in one case it's a scientific approach, principally, and it's written by someone who is possibly an authority. And when he says something it's the Bible, almost.

DR. B.: Well, I have my feelings about the literal use of the Bible, too.

MOTHER: I mean, it's different. A novel is just something that somebody thought up, and . . .

DR. B.: So are some scientific books. To me some scientific books are like the novel—something somebody else thought about, which stimulates me to do my own thinking. And I think Spock's book is a novel. Because a scientific treatise is characterized by the fact that it presents evidence. It is considered the requirement of scientific writing that you present your evidence separately from the inferences, and the conclusions you draw from it. Then you discuss your own conclusions critically. I don't know what your husband is studying . . .

132

MOTHER: Well, I've studied enough to know that myself.

DR. B.: All right. What did you study?

MOTHER: I studied economics.

DR. B.: Okay. But isn't that considered overall scientific procedure?

MOTHER: Yes.

DR. B.: And what, in economics, is Max Weber? He's considered a philosopher, not a scientist. Isn't that correct?

MOTHER: Yes.

DR. B.: Now, in a way philosophy can be much more stimulating because you don't have to accept or rely on someone else's data. You know that it's speculation, so it's a mere starting point for your own speculation. Isn't that all it is, the books of Max Weber? Do you accept my differentiating between these two types of economics?

MOTHER: Yes.

DR. B.: In the one kind of scientific writing where the evidence is given, there we learn facts. There's another kind of writing, and in economics I could mention Max Weber, or Mannheim or somebody like that; that's philosophy, that's speculation—and we know that it's meant to stimulate our own speculation. Now, from your reading of Spock, you must have seen that his way is obviously the second way. He doesn't present data carefully analyzed. He uses examples out of his wide experience and then speculates about them.

Now let's go on from there, because aggression is very important. Let's speculate about the statement which you rightly or wrongly attribute to Spock. It's obviously a speculative statement, because there's no evidence of what is better or what is worse—those are value judgments. It could be better or worse, for instance, depending on what kind of a child you want to have; or what kind of relationship you want to have to your child. But until we've stated that clearly, we can never say that this is better, and that is worse. So let's have the specific statement again, please.

MOTHER: Well, I had read . . . one of the things I read was that very often you will do something that makes the child angry, and it's a good idea to let the child yell at you, or hit you, or in some way obviously show his anger, even though it isn't socially approved of to do these things. But it's good to let him do it, because it's better for him to get it out of his system, so to speak, than to keep a grudge for a long time.

DR. B.: Yes, but do you all realize that we have now heard an entirely different statement than the first one?

MOTHER: Well, what did I say?

SECOND MOTHER: Do you mean you agree with this one?

DR. B: Well, I'm much more ready to agree with it than the first one.

MOTHER: Why? What's the difference?

SECOND MOTHER: The first time, you said that the authority found it perfectly all right for the child to strike, or hit out. But you didn't say anything about any other way of getting rid of his hostility.

MOTHER: Oh . . . that was in addition to . . . I mean, if he wanted to.

DR. B.: But that makes it an entirely different statement!

SECOND MOTHER: Well, isn't that what usually happens? The child wants to hit back, if he's been hit first.

DR. B.: Not necessarily, but let's analyze the statement. What is Spock trying to prevent? Let's start with the aim.

SECOND MOTHER: Well, I think he'd rather have the hostilities out in the open than suppressed.

DR. B.: So what is he first of all trying to prevent?

MOTHER: Guilt feelings . . .

DR. B.: No, no. [Turning] You said it a minute ago. "Suppression," he says. "Given a series of events, and given the fact that it's the mother who imposes the suppression, any suppression by the mother is undesirable." That's the premise on which he started, and with which I heartily agree. That you shouldn't suppress your child if you can help it. But now we understand the goal better. The goal is no longer the discharge of hostility, as you put it in your first statement, but the avoidance of suppression, which is an entirely different story.

MOTHER: You mean, in my first statement I indicated that the child, out of a clear blue sky, would try to strike out at his parents?

DR. B.: No, no. Not out of a blue sky. But your child, for one reason or another, is angry and he should be permitted to hit the parent because it's good for him to discharge hostility.

MOTHER: Oh, no. I didn't mean that.

DR. B.: Yes, but that's what you said. And it was quite clear you meant that, because we were talking about the discharge of hostility.

MOTHER: Well, the child was angry at the mother because the mother had done something that made him angry.

DR. B.: Obviously. And therefore he should be permitted to strike the mother because it's good for him to discharge hostility.

MOTHER: Yes.

DR. B.: That was obvious.

MOTHER: I'm just caught in a swamp of words!

DR. B.: Look, tell me if you see any differences between the following attitudes that a parent could take. The child is swearing, and the parent says, "I can fully understand that you're angry, but I wish you wouldn't use bad language"; that's one possibility. Another possibility is, "From your swearing I see that you're angry, but these dirty words don't tell me at all why you're angry, and therefore I haven't the slightest idea what we can do about it"; that's a second possibility. Another is, "Go ahead, you're angry. Swear at me."

Or I could just say, "Shut up!" Do you see what I mean?

The "Go ahead" means "By all means, spit it out," with encouragement to discharge hostility. The last way is suppression, and whether you later beat him or not is immaterial from my point of view. "Shut up!" when said forcefully enough by a parent to a child is an inducement to suppress his emotions. Correct? Or at least, not to express them. Do you follow? All right! Now as a good mother, what are you after, if the child is badly frustrated?

MOTHER: The reason.

DR. B.: Why?

MOTHER: So that you can do something about it.

DR. B.: That's right. And that's what we call a goal-directed action. So which is better? For the child to discharge hostility, or for you to set the stage for a goal-directed action? To avoid, or to remedy the situation? What do you think?

MOTHER: The question answers itself.

DR. B.: Yes, but apparently not. Because otherwise we wouldn't be discussing it. That's why we had to start from the beginning. You see, you gave me a statement by Spock as the statement of an authority, and with that I couldn't do a thing. But what I hope is that Spock meant it, and you will use it, as a starting point for speculation: what did this man have in mind?

Through speculation we arrived at the conclusion that what he had in mind was, "When confronted with even a violent expression of hostility on the one hand, and its forceful suppression on the other, I'm willing to settle for the first even to the extent of being hit by the child." In the second statement, which I understand is the more correct one, he was going out of his way to make a forceful statement against the suppression of emotions.

MOTHER: Well, that was the reason I brought it up. You said that children shouldn't be treated differently from adults. Now, if I have something against my husband, I don't go over and hit him just because I'm mad at him.

DR. B.: Some people do.

MOTHER: That's true . . .

DR. B.: What about your husband?

MOTHER: Oh, I'm bigger than him!

DR. B.: Why do you add that?

MOTHER: I don't think . . . there was no subconscious feeling.

DR. B.: Well, then, give us the conscious one. Don't start that with me; there you're sunk.

MOTHER: Well . . . anyway . . . going back to what we started with . . .

DR. B.: Fast retreat!

MOTHER: As I said, there's no slugging at home.

DR. B.: Up to the time that your child is about to hit you, according to Spock.

MOTHER: Yes. Now why should . . . I'm just developing these thoughts from what you said before, when you said that children should be treated as adults, and adults wouldn't hit each other . . .

DR. B.: No, not as adults. They should be treated as sensibly as you expect adults to treat one another. Because they *are* different; for example, they are more vulnerable, and have a shorter span of attention. But they have the same reasons and emotions that we do. After all, you won't use the same language, you won't have the same expectations. You see? Now I'm afraid I'm going to be quoted as saying that children should be treated as adults, which I didn't say. I only said we shouldn't claim a difference where there is none.

MOTHER: Okay, but I still want to get to the point where he's hitting the parents. What do you do then?

DR. B.: I'm against it, and that's why I haven't gotten around to it in the first place. I'm against children hitting their parents, because I'm against hitting; not because it's not nice, or because I'm such a pacifist, which I'm not. I don't think it's a crime to slap a child, or to spank him. I just think it's a relatively ineffective way to solve a problem. I think there are more effective ways, that's all. But I know that doesn't satisfy you.

MOTHER: Well, if they *have* hit you, what do you say about it? I'm still not sure that I get it.

DR. B.: Then you grab his hand and hold him off firmly. "I won't let you do that. I'm bigger than you are, and I won't let you do that." And then you try to find out why he's hitting in the first place. My point is that there's a great long stretch from suppressing hostility, which is bad like all suppressions, to condoning a physical attack against the parent. Or we should say, unnecessary suppressions are bad, because some suppression is always necessary.

What I strongly object to is the either/or proposition: either you let a child attack his parents physically or you suppress his hostilities. That's an alternative I will not accept. I think a child should be encouraged, when he feels hostile, to express that—but to express it, if at all possible, in terms that will sooner or later lead to an understanding, and hence to a remedy of the situation. On the other hand, if you just say to him, "Tell me when you're angry," and then don't do something about it, it means that "Tell me when you're angry" is just an empty gesture, and nothing is more devastating to children than when parents make empty gestures.

And don't think I make these stories up. I've known parents who said, "Tell mommy if you're angry, tell mommy," and then they tell, and tell, and tell, and nothing ever happens—which is much worse than suppressing it, because it's just a teasing of the child. If you really want the child to tell you, then you've got to do something about it when he tells you. Or at least try to.

And since you're human, when a child hits you it

hurts, if not your body, then your feelings. But if you're hurt you're in a poor position to help him find out. And if he can beat you up, then you're a poor protector, though a child needs to feel his parents can protect him even more than he needs to discharge his aggressions.

Now, how did this "Let your child beat you" come about? I can only guess, but my guess is there are two sources, both bad. The first is that because some parents used to beat their children into submission and this was bad, we want it never to happen again. But instead of concluding that beating others is bad, some decided that it's bad for parents to beat their kids but okay for kids to beat their parents. That's bad reasoning.

The other source is that some of us were beaten by our parents and then dreamed of beating them up in revenge. Now it seems that some grownups haven't outgrown such childish notions of revenge and still want to see parents beaten up by their children. And they want revenge so much that they don't mind it, even if it's their own child who beats them up. That's bad, because such a parent is still engaging in childish thinking and hence is in a bad position to help his child toward more mature thinking, reasoning, and action.

One last word about discharging aggression. If you're mad and discharge it by hitting, that's the end of it; otherwise it isn't a discharge. But if it's the end, then there's no reason to find out what made you mad in the first place, or what you can do to prevent such exasperating things from happening again in the future. So Johnny shoots at Charlie, and Charlie in anxiety or defense shoots back. So Johnny in defense shoots at Charlie and they never stop to think, "Gosh, aren't there better ways to spend an afternoon?"

4

What's Affection?

MOTHER: Today you promised we were going to discuss kissing . . . why you're against it.

DR. B.: Oh, no! I'm not against kissing. You'll have to make your question more specific if you want me to discuss it.

MOTHER: Well, teaching babies to kiss.

DR. B.: That's very hard to teach to a baby.

MOTHER: Kissing babies, then.

DR. B.: Ah! That's different. Though I'm afraid that whatever I say it's going to get around campus that I'm against kissing. Well, who wants to say something for it or against it? Or do I have to do all the talking?

SECOND MOTHER: What's the matter with kissing, assuming you don't kiss them on the mouth, or their hands, or any place that's apt to get into the mouth?

DR. B.: Well, your choice of a particular place is only a subdivision of a larger problem.

SECOND MOTHER: But we're supposed to show affection to a child.

DR. B.: Who said that? I never said you're "supposed to show affection."

SECOND MOTHER: Well, any authority you read advocates it.

DR. B.: I don't read authorities, and then do as they tell me. I read books that can start me thinking on my own.

MOTHER: Anyway, kissing isn't the only form of showing affection.

DR. B.: Look, can we start all over again? I think we've just been presented with something much more important than kissing, namely the problem of showing "affection." As for kissing babies, I think we should leave it where it belongs, to the political candidates. More important, it seems to me, is your statement that according to all the authorities you read, you're supposed to show affection. What do you think of that?

MOTHER: Well, the "affection" you show is supposed to be something natural, not something you just show because you're supposed to.

DR. B.: So either you have it, or you don't. What perturbs me is that you're supposed to show affection whether you have it or not.

MOTHER: Well, if you don't have it, then you certainly won't show it.

THIRD MOTHER: Oh, no! You're more apt to, if you don't have it.

DR. B.: Exactly!

THIRD MOTHER: Don't you have guilt feelings if you don't love your child?

DR. B.: Maybe ... and maybe you then try to fool yourself, your husband, the child, or the whole world.

THIRD MOTHER: Anyway, everybody has different ways of showing it. Some people are very demonstrative and go around kissing everybody, and some people never show it outwardly but really have deep inner feelings.

DR. B.: Well, I know you're all quite grown-up girls now, but has any of you ever been a child before? Yes? How many of you were children before you became adults?

[*Someone asks, "At what age?" and there is a loud burst of laughter.*]

DR. B.: Now those of you who were once children and can recall it—you must have had the experience of

141

being shown affection, by an aunt, or a great-aunt, who kissed you all over the place. What did you do with her?

MOTHER: I hated her, because she scared me. Well, it wasn't because she scared me, but because it was false.

DR. B.: And that's why they kissed you profusely; because they were trying to fool you. But being a child, you didn't like having your natural feelings distorted, so you drew back ... which was just a challenge to her to do it even more, but now aggressively so, because "by golly" ... Okay. Now where do we go from here?

THIRD MOTHER: Well, one thing I'm definitely against is this dutiful kissing. I've observed many parents who take their little children before they go to bed and they have to kiss daddy good night, and then mommy and then teddy bear, and any brothers or sisters in the family. I don't like this dutiful kissing.

DR. B.: Yes. I think we'd all agree that that isn't good. We can dismiss that because I think it's no problem for us here. I think the problem is this "showing of affection which is advocated by the experts."

SECOND MOTHER: Doctor Bettelheim, I think you're really twisting what I meant. I certainly didn't mean to imply that one should show affection to a child merely because it was advocated by an authority.

DR. B.: That's right; so what *should* one show?

SECOND MOTHER: Well, just one's own feelings.

DR. B.: That's right. And are the feelings always affectionate?

SECOND MOTHER: Oh, no, far from it!

DR. B.: Far from it. So what you then say is, that according to your interpretation, the experts advocate that you should show all your feelings as they occur. Is that a correct interpretation of what you meant to say?

SECOND MOTHER: Well, mostly ...

DR. B.: "Mostly" doesn't help us much.

SECOND MOTHER: No, I guess you can't show all your feelings either. You have to exercise some curbs.

DR. B.: I agree. But as you see, the statement is now without value. First we started out by saying you should show your affection, then that you should show all your feelings; and now we've concluded that you can't do that either, for obvious reasons. Because we don't have only positive emotions. But the experts don't often talk about what to do with our negative emotions, which is actually a much bigger problem.

So where do the experts leave us? Exactly where they should always leave us: beginning to think on our own. Now let's go back again to the statement that you ought to show affection for your child. What does it really mean?

MOTHER: Well, it means that your child needs to be shown that it's loved.

DR. B.: Yes, he needs that so that he'll know for sure that we love him. But how do you do it?

MOTHER: Well, it isn't always done by kissing; it's done by everything; by looking after him . . .

DR. B.: Such as?

MOTHER: Being consistent in your method of handling him.

DR. B.: That only shows you're consistent. Consistency only shows you're consistent; isn't that true? Sure, he needs to know that you're consistent in your affection for him, but consistency doesn't show affection.

MOTHER: Well, I don't know that it takes any time to show affection; if you have it, it's just there. I kiss my little girl when I hug her, and I just do it whenever I want to.

DR. B.: All right, but is that experienced by the child as affection? What does affection mean to a small child?

MOTHER: You fulfill her needs, whatever they happen to be.

DR. B.: That's right. Let's have an example.

MOTHER: Oh, you feed her if she's hungry; you hold her close to you.

DR. B.: What else do you do? How do you play with an infant?

MOTHER: Oh, cuddly games.

DR. B.: Fine. Could you possibly tell us how you recognize when your infant is very happy? What does she do?

MOTHER: Oh, she smiles ...

DR. B.: And gurgles, and coos, and spits occasionally when she gets too excited; isn't that what she does? All right, do they do that when you kiss them, or when you play with them?

MOTHER: They do it when they're played with.

DR. B.: Tell me ... by and large, when does your small child show a greater reaction of satisfaction, when you kiss them on the mouth or cheek or when you tickle them on the stomach, or hug or cuddle them, or whatever else it is that you do?

MOTHER: Well, of course, when I tickle her on the stomach.

DR. B.: So is the child responding more to the kissing, or to the playing in various ways?

SECOND MOTHER: Both ways.

DR. B.: Maybe, though I'm not so sure. You can demonstrate that you hardly ever get a smiling reaction from an infant if the mother only kisses him on the mouth or the cheek and doesn't also hug him. But you very often get it the other way around.

MOTHER: That depends pretty much on how you kiss the baby. If you kiss it on the back of the neck it tickles, and they like it.

DR. B.: Sure, but isn't that basically tickling? So you tickle with the mouth instead of the finger because it gives you more pleasure to tickle with the mouth.

MOTHER: But the baby likes it.

DR. B.: Oh sure, the baby likes to be tickled! In the

baby you will get exactly the same reaction whether you tickle with your finger or with your mouth.

MOTHER: Oh, I know I kiss for my pleasure and the baby likes it, too.

DR. B.: All right, so then you kiss for your own pleasure and not for the baby's sake, and that's all I was trying to show. The baby enjoys the tickling at least as much as the kissing. Now we understand that kissing is done for the pleasure of the mother and not for the pleasure of the baby; so far so good. But kissing gives the child an image for seeking pleasure which is far ahead of his age. Kissing normally comes in high school, as you know.

[Some low voices are heard, feeling unhappy, expressing doubt at this statement.]

DR. B.: Through your image, because of what you do, you start a premature, because adult, erotic response, which is far beyond the child's age. To the child about whom we were talking, it is at first just a tickling; whether you tickle with the finger or the mouth is immaterial. But soon the child begins to wonder, "Why does mommy do it with her mouth?" when a hand is obviously more convenient for the stimulation.

MOTHER: Not only that, but they sense that you enjoy it.

DR. B.: And so they want to copy you. In this way you encourage a premature sexuality in the child. It is characteristic of a baby to respond with generalized, not specific, reactions. The baby does not react with the language of his eyes or his mouth alone, as you know, but his whole body. That response is the one in line with his age. As we grow older, our reactions become more and more specialized in all areas, including the sexual area. This is how development proceeds. And as much as we can prematurely push a child into taking care of himself, into dressing himself, we can prematurely push him into kissing. Now one thing about kissing is that once you start it you cannot stop it so easily.

SECOND MOTHER: What about the kissing to make something well? That becomes a kind of ritual after a while.

DR. B.: You can as easily blow on it to make it well! Why not the ritual of blowing? After all, it hurts because it's hot, and if you blow on it, that cools the skin.

MOTHER: Well, just during the last few days our child has begun to react to the phrase "Give me a kiss." And she'll lick us, that's what she does. She doesn't kiss me as often as she kisses her father. Probably because he gets a bigger bang out of it than I do. Now she's fourteen months old, and I'm wondering . . . are we forcing her into premature sexuality?

DR. B.: I think you do, though "sexuality" is an awfully big word to use about a fourteen-month-old child. So let's not exaggerate. All I wanted you to understand was the principle. A child should not express his liking of a parent in an adult way, such as by kissing, but in his own childish way.

MOTHER: Of course we've encouraged it because we thought it was cute. I know she shows her affection in other ways; she'll come up to us and put her arms around our legs.

DR. B.: Well, that's fine. Kissing, as you know, in the normal sex relations is a preliminary to necking, and to petting, and then to intercourse. The question is: do you continuously want to have these first preliminaries with your child, so that they'll be tempted to have intercourse when they get to their teens?

[*Sounds of surprise, disbelief, and disapproval*]

MOTHER: Well, would that naturally follow?

DR. B.: Nothing follows naturally or with necessity

from it. But you have started it. I don't say that anything will follow, but is that enough reason to begin?

MOTHER: You mean they can actually be stimulated by a kiss?

DR. B.: *You* most certainly are. Isn't that why you do it?

MOTHER: Well, so is stroking, for that matter.

DR. B.: Yes, but stroking is not so concentrated, not so sexual, at least not usually.

MOTHER: Well, does that include hugging the baby?

DR. B.: No, because that's nonspecific, and that's what I've been trying to drive at. As long as you don't get a greater kick out of one area of the body than the other, then it's perfectly all right. To the child, if you disregard eating or sucking, the mouth is a part of the body like any other; like the nose, or the arm, or the hand. If you treat is as such, no overwhelming feelings are created.

MOTHER: But kissing is also a generalized social practice. Like the kissing of animals, and dutiful kissing between females; or like the relationship to one's mother and daughter, or other relatives. It has many other general usages.

DR. B.: Let me just remind you again of how you felt as children. How did you feel when you were kissed by adults, if you can still remember it? What emotions were evoked in you, positive or negative? Weren't they much stronger, more powerful when kissed on the mouth, or when *you* were asked to kiss? If so, then the question is: do you want to get an emotional response from your child based on a quasi-sexual stimulus, or as the result of a total relationship? You're the boss of your child, so you can have it either way. I cannot tell you what you should do; I can only show you what consequences your actions are apt to have.

SECOND MOTHER: It's funny. When the child gets to go to school, kissing and showing affection to school mates is looked down on and ridiculed, and that gets the child confused.

DR. B.: No, the child is not confused. Maybe an example from the Orthogenic School may help. There we get children who are among the most affection-starved children, who have been, or feel themselves totally rejected by the world. But even though these children think that affection is totally out of reach for them, we manage, with extremely rare exceptions, to give nearly every one of them the feeling that they're liked, and very much so. And this without ever kissing one of them.

As a matter of fact, once when a beginning counselor had the bad sense to kiss one of these children, and not even on the mouth, his reaction was, if you ladies will excuse me, a four-letter word telling her what she should do to him, or with him. This was his instantaneous reaction. Sure, he was a child of nature, not practiced in the social conventions. That's why he was immediately able to show his emotional reaction. He was a six-year-old boy, by the way.

MOTHER: Well, does that mean there was any definite physical excitation in him?

DR. B.: Yes! Measurably so!

MOTHER: But it would have to be beyond a certain age when the child realized, wouldn't it?

DR. B.: No, the mouth is, as you know, a particularly sensitive spot. Sensations created there by friction are much greater, are much more excited than in other parts of the body. What you do is to excite your child there more than at most other spots; more than with your kiss on the neck. As a matter of fact, your kiss on his mouth is probably not so exciting . . .

SECOND MOTHER: But *his* kiss!

DR. B.: That's right, and his copying you. For this reason I am much more doubtful of the child kissing the parent than I am of the parent kissing the child. But since the first is very often the consequence of the

148

second, it seems wiser to draw limitations around the first.

SECOND MOTHER: But how do you go about this? What should your attitude be in the home as your child grows older? You can't always avoid kissing the child; you kiss your husband in front of the child, and sometimes you just naturally pick the child up and kiss it.

DR. B.: Well, don't you want to give the child the idea that that's something a husband and the wife do with one another?

SECOND MOTHER: Sure.

DR. B.: All right, then that's what I'd say; that's what married people do with one another.

SECOND MOTHER: But won't he feel rejected?

DR. B.: Good lord, is he married to you? We talk about the Oedipus complex, and all the difficulties around it, and then we push the children into it by assuming that all the things we do with our husband we should also do with our son so that he won't feel rejected.

SECOND MOTHER: But how can you prevent the child from kissing you?

DR. B.: I don't know; I don't think you have to if you don't teach it to them first. When children start in nursery or kindergarten, they see other children do it, and sometimes they'll try. My own children did that and I accepted it. I certainly didn't reject it; but it wasn't something I in particular cherished. I would rather they hugged me or climbed on me, or something like that. They knew that, and they liked it better, too.

Still, the kissing was something they had to experiment with because they'd seen it in others; but the hugging or the carrying they liked much better. And this is my point: if you offer a child a kiss or a piggy-back ride and the child is not conditioned to the importance of kissing, he'll take the piggy-back ride. So what do children really like?

149

SECOND MOTHER: Then you'd adopt a nonenthusiastic attitude, or an off-hand attitude?

DR. B.: Well, you cannot adopt an attitude; either you have an attitude or you don't. All I can recommend is that you follow your own attitudes, but not without examining them from time to time. Some insights that we gain change our attitudes. And your attitude will change, not because I have told you something, but only if and when it becomes your inner conviction that your child really enjoys a piggy-back ride more than a kiss. Then if you want to do something very nice you will give him a piggy-back ride, because you know he enjoys it more, rather than the kiss you enjoy more. But it'll work only if that's an inner conviction to which you react, and which motivates you. And that's that.

FOURTH MOTHER: Can we go over to something else now?

DR. B.: Yes, sure.

FOURTH MOTHER: Just recently my little boy discovered what the difference is between boys and girls, and it was contrary to what I expected.

DR. B.: Yes, we're all prepared for one thing, and then it's not what they do.

FOURTH MOTHER: Well, that's exactly what happened. I was keeping a little girl from across the hall for an hour or so, and Mark, my little boy who's two and a half, has just learned about urinating and wanted to go to the bathroom. So I took him in, and he was standing up, of course. Then the little girl wanted to go, too, so I started to put her on, and he said, "No," she should stand up. So one thing led to another and . . .

DR. B.: Now there you'll have to be more specific.

FOURTH MOTHER: Well, I said that Janey can't stand up, she's a little girl; she sits down. And then he said, "Why does she sit down?" So I said, "Janey doesn't have a penis." That was all I said, but he was very perplexed. Incidentally, he has a little sister now and apparently hasn't observed it; or if he has, he's made no sign of it.

DR. B.: In the little sister he still hopes it will grow; that she may still acquire one.

FOURTH MOTHER: Well, that may very well be, because he's commented that she doesn't have any teeth.

DR. B.: Yes. In books they call that displacement upwards.

FOURTH MOTHER: Of course, I did tell him that she'd get teeth eventually, but I know he was worried about it.

DR. B.: Well, in such a case and since he seemed to be worried, I'd just ask, "Is there any other difference between her and you?"

FOURTH MOTHER: Oh, you bring it up yourself? That was just what I didn't know.

DR. B.: I don't say you should start anything, but since he talks about the teeth which are a relatively small part of the body compared to the penis, I'd bring it up. Since he's intelligent, has good eyesight, and has observed the absence of teeth, we must assume he has also observed the absence of the other.

FOURTH MOTHER: But what if a little boy just announces that a little girl *has* a penis?

DR. B.: Is this a theoretical question or a practical one?

FOURTH MOTHER: Well, what happened was that he looked a little disturbed ... and my reaction was that he was worried for Janey. So I said, "All little girls don't have penises, and Janey's a little girl; every little boy has a penis, and you're a little boy." But since then he wants to sit down like girls do, and he obviously worries because he *does* have a penis. I've assumed it's because of the new baby; she doesn't have one, and obviously she has certain advantages.

DR. B.: That's a very good guess. Maybe he's ready for nursery school. Have you thought about it?

FOURTH MOTHER: Well, I was wondering if I should have sent him this fall.

DR. B.: Yes, I think nursery school will take care of the standing up.

FOURTH MOTHER: I've also explained to him that his father has a penis, and things like that, but there aren't enough little boys around, that's the whole trouble. In the meantime, should I just keep at it, till about the time he goes to nursery school?

DR. B.: Yes. You can explain it very gently, without rubbing it in; and if he wants to sit down, let him sit down! Or let him stand up if he wants to.

FOURTH MOTHER: I just want him to feel happy with what he is.

DR. B.: Yes, but he has doubts about it. And he has doubts for the reasons you correctly explained: that girls seem to be better off, since the girl baby gets more of mommy's time, and so forth. We have to counteract that by building him up in these other ways, as you say, by his masculinity and what boys and men can do.

But you see (*turning back to the group*) here you have an answer to the initial question, "How do you show affection to a child?" This is the way to show affection, and not by kissing. As a matter of fact, it shows it much better than even hugging. All the hugging in the world will not "show" your child affection, it will only show him that you have a need to do something about your emotions.

You've all known these admirers who're always around when you're beautifully dressed and in the best of moods, but who lose interest when you're gloomy and the sparkle is gone. You know very well that these first lovers aren't good enough. They only *show* affection but don't feel it; or they show it only because (or when) they're in love, but not when you may need it most. Someone who's truly interested in you can be even more interested in you and in helping you when you have a problem to solve . . . when you're in a bad mood. Which also applies to anger, incidentally.

It's when you have to say, "No" to the child that he needs you much more than he needs the approval you read about in books. If they learn a new word and you give them approval, that's all right, but they don't really need it very badly. For the first words, yes; but after a time they know they're acquiring something that's good to have anyway, whether you approve it or not. But if you have to say, "No" to them, or have to restrict them, that's when they need your understanding and affection.

To discuss urination or the sex differences with your child when he's perturbed about them, that's proof in action, not a "show" of your interest or concern. A child reacts most to your helpfulness, the degree to which you help him particularly in his moments of stress. That's how he builds up his opinions and learns about your attitudes, and not by what the books call a show of affection such as cuddling and so on, which is gratuitous and all right, if it comes in addition. But if he gets that without the other, you appear only as a fake or cheat. It means that you give it where the child doesn't need it, or doesn't need it much. And where your child needs it most, you withold it; and that is a tease.

There is so much confusion nowadays about this "showing of affection"—fortunately not yet in action, but in thinking—that I thought the most constructive service I could render you, once it came up, was to concentrate on it for this meeting. Next time we're going to concentrate entirely on your really pressing problems, including Christmas shopping if you like.

5

The Purpose of Pleasure

MOTHER: I'd like to hear you talk more about the use of the pacifier. I'm all confused about how you use them and why.

DR. B.: Preferably in the mouth!

MOTHER: Well, I have a month-old boy, and a little girl who's almost two. We gave the older one the pacifier, too, when she was that little, but we only used it when we couldn't bear to sit up any more. Well, she doesn't take the pacifier now; she uses the bottle instead. But she won't go to bed without it; she uses that as a pacifier.

DR. B.: That's conjecture, but go ahead.

MOTHER: Well, what I'd like to know is, can you develop the need to suck more? Let me put it that way. Maybe if I give it to the baby he'll want it all the time. Because that's the feeling I have with Laurie; that maybe she'll want it all the time!

[Burst of laughter]

DR. B.: Oh, she might proceed to the beer bottle later on. The development is from the milk bottle to the pop bottle to the coke bottle to the beer bottle. Sometimes it ends up with whiskey, and that's what we call human progress.

MOTHER: But there are times when I can't readily attend to him, and either I have to let him cry or else give him the pacifier. Because I have to attend to my girl. So I was just wondering if I should give it to him freely.

DR. B.: What speaks for it, and what speaks against it?

MOTHER: Well, this is how I feel about it. If I can give it to him freely, that gives me a lot of freedom, too. So I'm wondering: if it doesn't hurt him to have it a lot, well then, I wouldn't mind a bit.

DR. B.: Yes. Now I understand your question, and I think what you're asking is very important: is the pacifier something undesirable if it's offered to the child just to give the mother free time?

MOTHER: I do try to avoid giving it except when it's necessary.

DR. B.: Well, there again we get into deep water. When is it necessary?

MOTHER: Oh, if I have certain kinds of work. For instance, if I have to change Laurie. But it's hard to make the decision.

DR. B.: That's right. And that's why I take it up for discussion. For one set of reasons we can give the child a pacifier if he's unhappy, or doesn't sleep and the mother gets tired of sitting up, or holding him, or what not. For other reasons, the pacifier is very useful to just put in the child's mouth for the convenience of the mother. Now, how do we know what's the right amount, or how much is all right?

SECOND MOTHER: I started giving my child a pacifier when she was only about ten days old because she screamed all night, every night. I found out that the pacifier stopped her screaming. We didn't give it to her when we thought she was hungry; we just gave it to her at night.

DR. B.: All right, girls, tell me something that interests me. When I started these meetings, which is now three years ago if I'm not mistaken, there was violent disagreement about whether to use the pacifier or not. Now what is this? Have you heard that I'm for the pacifier, and now you're afraid to say what you think? Or has the world really changed so much?

[*A buzz of laughter and comment*]

THIRD MOTHER: I've never used one. Why should it be necessary to use one at all?

FOURTH MOTHER: Well, that's what I should think. After all, there are a number of substitutes. You could give the child a drink of water, possibly, or lay it on its stomach. Have you tried that?

MOTHER: Oh, I do all those things. It's only maybe after two or three hours past the feeding that I resort to the pacifier.

FOURTH MOTHER: Well ... I don't know. I myself have never used one and I haven't had an undue amount of trouble.

DR. B.: Yes, but that's no argument, because that's been told us since time immemorial: I spank my child, and I put him in the corner, and I lock him in the closet, and I never had any bad results.

FOURTH MOTHER: But why start at all? If the child doesn't know what it is, he won't demand it.

DR. B.: That's right! If the child doesn't know what democracy is, why teach him democracy! He won't demand it; he won't know what it is.

FOURTH MOTHER: Well, I think democracy and ... that ... are two different things.

DR. B.: Why? The principle applies: if he doesn't know what is it, he won't miss it, so why teach it to him in the first place? Why teach democracy to begin with?

THIRD MOTHER: Well, I've never used a pacifier. When my child seemed to be hungry, I used a bottle with small holes that almost amounts to a pacifier.

DR. B.: So if it amounts to a pacifier, why not a pacifier?

THIRD MOTHER: It doesn't make any difference with

me except that he was hungry all the time and he was sucking so much in the eating business. I don't see why a child who wants to eat a lot must necessarily have any substitute, like another pacifier or something like that.

SECOND MOTHER: Anyway, how do you know when your child needs a pacifier, or when he needs to suck at the age of one month?

FOURTH MOTHER: Some pediatricians say to just give it a wallop of phenobarbital and put them to bed for a while.

SECOND MOTHER: That's different. Sometimes the child needs some phenobarbital and sometimes it needs a pacifier.

DR. B.: Now, just a minute. The child doesn't need phenobarbital.

SECOND MOTHER: Well, I was thinking of some young babies who have trouble with sleep, or are sick, or something like that.

DR. B.: Oh sure, sick babies need medicine. If he's sick and his sickness requires phenobarbital, then he needs it. But you can't say a well child needs phenobarbital.

MOTHER: This is a little off the subject of the pacifier, but it's about the sucking.

DR. B.: Anything about sucking is in order tonight.

MOTHER: Do children vary a good bit in their sucking needs?

DR. B.: Yes. Children vary in all respects, including the amount of sucking they need.

MOTHER: Well, would you call it a desire? Do babies have desires?

DR. B.: Yes, strangely enough, they have desires.

MOTHER: Well, what about these desires?

DR. B.: I don't know. I'm not ready to talk. I want to hear more from you. If I were ready to talk, I would talk, believe me! But please, only those who haven't been through this with me before, because the new group wants to learn something, too.

MOTHER: Well, it seems to me that the pacifier is the mother's interpretation of the child's need.

DR. B.: What do you mean by that?

MOTHER: Well, that children who live in well-adjusted homes, where the mother is calm and there's a good mother-child relationship, they don't seem to need a pacifier.

DR. B.: How many homes do you know that are well-adjusted, and where the mother is always calm?

SECOND MOTHER: And how can a mother establish a good mother-child relationship with a newborn baby?

DR. B.: Just a moment. What is adjustment? I don't use these terms but I get them fed back by my students and now I get them from you. If you're going to use fancy terms, you'll have to explain what you mean. What is adjustment?

MOTHER: Adjustment?

DR. B.: Yes ... you spoke to me of where the mother and child are well-adjusted to one another.

MOTHER: Well, it's a relationship, I guess.

DR. B.: What's a relationship? Does it fall from the sky?

MOTHER: No, it's between the mother and child.

DR. B.: And how does it come about?

MOTHER: Oh, the way you take care of the child.

DR. B.: And the way the child takes care of you?

MOTHER: Well, that could be.

DR. B.: Don't be ridiculous ... excuse me ... how can a baby take care of you?

MOTHER: Well, I think the baby does take care of its mother—not physically, of course ...

DR. B.: Then this poor baby has to take care of its mother in its infancy. Well then, what is adjustment? You've all used the term; what does it mean "to adjust"?

MOTHER: It means to get along in any situation.

DR. B.: That's right. Now, if you meet somebody on the streetcar, let's say, do you adjust to him?

MOTHER: [*Shakes her head*]

DR. B.: Why not?

MOTHER: It's a temporary situation.

DR. B.: That's right, it's a temporary situation. Well then, what does adjustment take?

MOTHER: It takes time.

DR. B.: A long time . . . that's right! Adjustment is a mutual process between two or more persons that takes time. Yes? You can't do it in ten days. Just think of your husband! And what else does an adjustment presuppose?

MOTHER: Well, a close contact.

DR. B.: A close contact between whom?

MOTHER: The mother and the child.

DR. B.: But if we say that two people adjust, what do we expect of each one of them?

MOTHER: That there's a give and take.

DR. B.: That's right. And that one doesn't entirely adjust to the other. That we don't call adjustment; that we call . . . ?

MOTHER: Tyranny.

DR. B.: That's right, or something like it. Now! Can there be a mutual adjustment between mother and child?

MOTHER: No.

DR. B.: Because the child has no freedom. He can cry, but he cannot specify for what. If you offer a pacifier he can take it or leave it. If you withold it, there's nothing he can do. So you see, your initial statement, that there can be a wonderful adjustment, is just not so.

MOTHER: Perhaps I used the wrong words.

DR. B.: No, you used the wrong thoughts. Because if you say, "My child adjusts to me," that's a polite way of saying, "My child does what I jolly well want him to do." But that would be too unpleasant for us to think,

159

so we use these polite terms, to fool ourselves about what we are doing with the child.

You can't talk of "a good adjustment between mother and child" because there is no such thing; because a child doesn't have that much freedom. Nor can such an adjustment be established when the baby is born or in its first weeks of life. The arrival of a new baby in the family is upsetting to the balance of the whole family. And you are such a saint, and your husband is such a saint, and the baby is such a perfect baby, that you can adjust to each other.

Let's be realistic. As much as we may like the baby and want it, the arrival of a child presents all family members with the most difficult problems of a changed way of life. Suddenly you can't sleep through the night anymore, and you know what that means. Some infants cry a great deal and need all your attention, and what not. It's a terribly difficult problem. Probably, next to marriage, the most difficult of all.

In a marriage there's some preparation. You go out together, you spend more and more time together, it's a much slower process. And both partners, supposedly, have some chance to influence the adjustment, the marriage. The baby has no chance at all; therefore, it cannot influence the relationship, or at least for a while. Now to come back to the pacifier, which the baby can't say that it wants or doesn't want. The question is, why should the baby need it?

THIRD MOTHER: Well, my baby's three months old, and he eats a lot when he eats, but he still keeps right on sucking his thumb.

DR. B.: And are you a calm, well-adjusted mother?

THIRD MOTHER: No-o-o . . . I'm not. I nurse him part time, and I give him the bottle part time, but he still sucks his thumb so loud you can hear it in the next room. And I don't know whether it's good for him to suck his thumb or not.

DR. B.: Well, there's not a thing you can do about it, anyway.

THIRD MOTHER: Does that mean there's a problem there? I mean, would it help if I used a pacifier?

DR. B.: Well, I think the pacifier is usually easier to keep clean, it's softer, and they don't get callouses on their thumbs. That's why I'm for the pacifier. Sure, the thumb or the finger is an equally good instrument to suck on. But, if we agree on sucking, which we haven't yet, I'm in favor of the pacifier for the reasons I've just given; it's also better formed in accordance with the sucking movement and causes less deformation of the gums.

FOURTH MOTHER: Well, there's one thing I want to know, Dr. B. Does it serve a very real purpose?

DR. B.: Does smoking have any real purpose, apart from the cigarette industry?

FOURTH MOTHER: Well, yes ... I think so. Not absolutely, but to the individual who's the smoker, I think it does.

DR. B.: That's right. And what is the purpose?

FOURTH MOTHER: Well, relaxation.

DR. B.: All right. So relaxation is the real purpose?

FOURTH MOTHER: Yes.

DR. B.: Then why don't you apply that to the pacifier? You said it. I didn't put it in your mouth!

FOURTH MOTHER: Well, I wanted to know. I think I have my own notions ...

DR. B.: If you think that relaxation for those who need relaxation is a good purpose, and if you say that sucking or smoking serves this purpose, and serves it better, let's say, than morphine or whiskey, then why not? If somebody needs something soothing, I think we could agree that chewing gum, as against drinking whiskey, is preferable.

Now if you agree to that, then we have to ask: what possible means of relaxation can we give to an infant who seems to need relaxation? I'd say that to force a

161

pacifier on a child who never cries and is always perfectly happy, that would be silly, only I don't know any babies who never cry. But given these facts, why do you ask me? If you think there's a baby who's occasionally uncomfortable and seems to need to relax, and if you have no objection to chewing gum as compared to drinking whiskey, why not? Why not give it the pacifier?

FOURTH MOTHER: I see no reason why not. I see no objection to it. But I very often gave my baby a drink of water, which is the same thing as a pacifier. But he got a drink of water.

DR. B.: No, it isn't! Why do you give him water if he doesn't want water?

FOURTH MOTHER: Well, apparently that satisfied him.

DR. B.: How do you know? How do you know that the baby wouldn't have been equally satisfied with the pacifier, and wouldn't have overloaded his intestinal tract with unnecessary water?

FOURTH MOTHER: Well, I think that sometimes they want it. It seemed to satisfy him.

DR. B.: But why do you feel it's preferable?

FOURTH MOTHER: I don't say it's preferable, but I can't say exactly my reasons.

DR. B.: Well, if, let's assume, that to chew one substance (like gum) is just to chew, while another substance (like whiskey) includes substances that have nothing to do with the need . . . which would you prefer? What is more rational, more sensible to do?

FOURTH MOTHER: Well, whatever would serve your purpose.

DR. B.: Alone! And without any extraneous substances added. And while it's possible that the child does want water, we haven't found that out yet. All we know is that the child wants to suck. Why, then, for the child to enjoy sucking, must he also ingest water? That's my question. It just isn't reasonable. If the baby might want to suck and not want the water, why do you say, "I give him water instead of the pacifier," without at least finding out?

FOURTH MOTHER: Well, I agree with you there.

DR. B.: You shouldn't say that, because you don't act on it, and therefore you must have good reasons. If you give the baby the water bottle instead of the pacifier, you must have good reasons. And to save time, because it's getting late, let me suggest what those reasons might be. They belong to our puritanic American tradition: If it serves a practical purpose, you may indulge in the sucking. If it's only for enjoyment, it's bad and should not be permitted. So because of our puritanic traditions, the child has to eat before he's able to enjoy sucking, although he doesn't want food at the moment, and doesn't need it; although it's an unnecessary thing in the intestinal tract.

We get this again and again. I see children in my work ... one child is still forty pounds overweight, because he was so brought up that he can only chew if he eats. Eating is right, but chewing without eating is wrong. So this poor child, who has a great need to chew for reasons of his own, has to be forty pounds overweight until he can hardly move. But that's all right! As long as he eats, he can chew away.

FOURTH MOTHER: Well, even school teachers stop the children from chewing gum.

DR. B.: That's very simple. For those who were not permitted to enjoy chewing, the sight of other people chewing is a painful experience. Since they cannot permit it in themselves, they have to stop it in others.

FOURTH MOTHER: Well, wouldn't chewing on toys, except for the hardness, satisfy the need?

DR. B.: No, it wouldn't. Because it answers the need, but doesn't give the pleasure. There it is again; he may chew, but it mustn't be pleasant. Nor can I see why [*to the fourth mother*] the poor child, in order to enjoy sucking, must also ingorge water. You still haven't given me the real reasons.

THIRD MOTHER: Well, if the child doesn't get the pacifier, and wants to suck on something, won't he eventually take to the thumb? So what's the objection to the thumb?

DR. B.: I don't object!

THIRD MOTHER: Well, what about letting the child suck the thumb instead of the pacifier?

DR. B.: I told you why! Because it's cleaner and softer. Neither does it incapacitate the child in his movements. The small infant especially is constantly having to choose between playing with something or holding the thumb in his mouth.

SECOND MOTHER: Well, I was going to say that my older boy has always sucked his thumb, and at this point it really looks peculiar; he has quite a large callous.

DR. B.: Well, that will straighten out later on, I hope. But why have the callous on the fingers? Why inhibit the use of the right hand, the strong hand, which should be free for creeping, moving, or playing? With the pacifier he can move and play as he wishes.

FOURTH MOTHER: Wouldn't a pacifier stimulate the gastric juices and cause some stomach discomfort?

DR. B.: Certainly. But so would thumb sucking, only more so, because it's bigger. That's another reason why the thumb is much worse. But I still don't object to the thumb. Anyway, don't fool yourself; every child will suck his thumb, too, even if you give him the pacifier.

FIFTH MOTHER: Can I change the subject, Dr. B? My question is about toys. I don't want to spend any money without first asking you ...

[*Burst of laughter*]

DR. B.: Finally we have a real problem! Well ... we haven't really solved the pacifier problem because you haven't really told me what your objection is ... your inner objections, not your intellectual agreement. And if you don't deal with those, you don't achieve anything. I would like to have heard one creditable argument against the pacifier! Because there's no doubt that at least half of you have misgivings about using it. And if you have any misgivings, you might as well not use it at all.

The pacifier is not a prescription, you know. It doesn't effect miracles; it's only the pacifier plus the right attitude. The pacifier alone doesn't do you much good. But I'm afraid that's exactly what we've reached here. We've driven underground the opposition to the pacifier, and it hasn't done you any good at all. Maybe next time. Okay?

In this discussion one difficulty came out quite clearly. The mothers could not accept giving the child the pleasure of sucking when it was not nutritive. But there were other emotions not discussed that interfered with the group's ability to accept the pacifier as a simple means of providing the child with body comfort. Since they were not brought out in the open, at least two of them should be mentioned for my readers.

First, the modern mother seems to feel sometimes that she should be able to provide all pleasure satisfactions for her infant, or at least enough of them so that he need not seek any more. So if the child sucks his thumb, that's bad enough, but to offer him a pacifier seems like a declaration of failure. The second and related feeling seems to be that if the child seeks additional satisfaction, he should seek it from the mother and not provide it for himself. There is a basic mistrust of the mother-child relation underlying this hesitation to let the child seek pleasure from his own body, as if it might lead the child to neglect his relations with the mother.

I referred in the discussion to the puritanic

attitude that demands that pleasure should not be sought for itself and not in bodily comfort. Here I might add that while this particular content of puritanism is fortunately on the wane, it appears that a deeper puritanism is still with us. It demands of the mother that she be so perfect a provider of mothering that no need of the child will remain unsatisfied by her. Thus the child's seeking pleasure on his own is seen as proof that the mother is inadequate and hence a bad mother; and therefore the child's activity is obnoxious to the mother.

If I may add a comment, because it seems pertinent: we have come a long way in having learned to try to protect our children from pain and unnecessary frustration. But we stand barely at the beginning of the corollary realization: that protection from pain or discomfort still leaves the individual in a void so long as he is not also helped to find pleasure in the process of living.

IV

What Kind of Child Do You Want?

1

Cause and Consequence

FATHER: I don't know if I can phrase this right, but we've always been concerned with the general idea of how much restraint can you, and should you, introduce in the child's life with respect to the people around him or the objects in his life, and so on.

DR. B.: Well, that goes back to the more basic issue of what kind of a child you want to have. What kind of a person do you want your child to be when he grows up? Not that you'll get him made to order, you know. But it seems to me that if you're a reasonable parent, you should realize that whatever steps you take will have consequences. After all, the important things aren't the steps, they're the consequences. Wouldn't you agree?

Therefore, it seems to me that the amount of restraint you impose will have consequences; the relative absence of restraint will have consequences; and whatever you do, you'll have done your share to make a different person. That's why I can't really answer your question.

It would be extremely presumptuous on my part to tell you what kind of a child you should have, or what kind of a person you should want your child to grow up to be. That's why some of you have gotten tired of the books on how to raise children. Because the books proceed as if there were a model person to strive for, and if you just do this and that you will get such a person. Firstly, it isn't true; you don't get that person.

And secondly, I think it would be a terrible world if everybody grew up to be alike. So unless you tell me what kind of a person you'd like your child to be, I can't tell you whether you should use a lot of restraint or a little bit of restraint, or how to use it, and so forth.

FATHER: Well, maybe if we can boil down our definition of what kind of a child you want ... essentially I believe it would be a child who'd be capable of making adjustments to a changing world. That is, a flexible child.

DR. B.: How flexible? When Hitler comes, he's for Hitler? And the next day, when Stalin comes, he's for Stalin? Is that the kind of flexibility you want?

FATHER: No, no! Definitely not.

DR. B.: All right. So you see that just in a few seconds of talking you've already found out that your statement was too vague. Therefore, please don't expect me to give you back an equally vague statement about using restraint or not using restraint. That I cannot do. But if you could tell me what kind of a person you want your child to be, I think I can help you a little bit to decide which means of education, of training, are entirely out of the question, which attitudes might be more apt to produce the kind of child you do want, and which means of education might lead to something in between. But first you have to answer for yourself, and not vaguely but pretty concisely, the question of what kind of a child you want to have. Now you don't have to agree with what I'm saying, but if it doesn't make sense to you, I wish you would question it.

FATHER: No, it does make sense. Except that when you put it that way, then it's a question of not having gotten far enough with the question of what kind of a child I do want.

DR. B.: Yes, but how can you decide the question of restraint or not restraint independent of that? That's what I'm trying to show you. And the question of when to use restraint—of when to use certain educational means, and when not to use them—is a very central issue in rearing a child. But I think it depends on the kind of child you want to have, because that's exactly where a parent *can* make a difference. About the external appearance, there is very little he can do. About the native intelligence, or other natural endowment, he can do very little. But education—that's the only means a parent can use in order to change—or I should say, to influence—whatever is given by nature.

FATHER: Well, I think I'll just have to break the question down in my mind, in terms of these things. That is, you've brought up one question. It's a cultural-political question essentially, maybe an economic one, in terms of Hitler and Stalin.

DR. B.: Well, I took an exaggerated and silly example in order to tell you in an obvious way that your statement in its general form doesn't make much sense.

FATHER: Well, I took it this way: that our society itself as it stands today has its own strength; and that our laws, or whatever it may be, defines it.

DR. B.: Do you know the percentage of citizens who've never broken the law?

FATHER: No, I don't.

DR. B.: It's very small.

FATHER: Then the restraint is completely on the social side. Is that an argument proving that the law is the restraining factor? Or is it the people's morality that's restraining? Is it one thing or the other?

DR. B.: I don't know. I think a good point can be made for the restraining influence of the law. Now, some people get caught in the law, you understand. But by and large it's enforced only when public feeling is on the side of the law. And when public feeling is against it, then the law is not enforced. So there the law is not the restraining influence, but the attitude of the public. You see, I can turn it back to you and say that your son or your daughter will soon be part of the public. Therefore, he will not only be restrained by the laws but will also help to decide which laws should be enforced, which should be changed, which should be neglected, and so on.

FATHER: Well, there's at least that restraint imposed. I suppose the public in general decides what will be the restraint on the child in terms of its social development. So it's a real thing, public feeling.

DR. B.: That's right. Now ... do you want a child who is run by public opinion?

FATHER: Well ... I'm afraid I can't pin this down to particulars.

DR. B.: All right, but then I cannot help you. I only want to make you aware that whatever educational means you exercise will have their influence on the child. The more radical they are, the more radical the influences will be for better or for worse. It doesn't necessarily mean that the influence will be in the direction you want it to be, because as you know, certain forces evoke counterforces. But by and large I would think that the best thing you can do is to think this problem through, first.

FATHER: Well, let me ask an extreme question. Do you think that a situation where the parent imposes no restraint at all would be a good situation?

DR. B.: Excuse me ... what is your special field?

FATHER: I'm in bacteriology.

DR. B.: You would never ask ... excuse me ... such a stupid question in bacteriology. Look. I'll turn the question back to you and you'll see immediately that you'd go about things much more sensibly if you were setting up an experiment in bacteriology.

FATHER: I'm just thinking in terms of behavior or attitudes that I've seen. And it appears just as stupid to me when I see ... although ... well, perhaps there is some sense to using no restraint ...

DR. B.: Look ... what do you mean by no restraint?

You wouldn't talk about bacteria as if they exist or live nowhere. You would know immediately that they exist in a certain setting, in a certain environment. That these certain conditions make all the difference, such as temperature. In a certain temperature they grow, in another they don't. But of your child you talk as if he were being raised in a vacuum. There are certain things given for this child, just as in the laboratory certain conditions are given. For instance, you talk to the child. Well, the very fact that you talk to him and are not mute already exercises a certain influence on the child—doesn't it? Now: what do you mean by restraint?

FATHER: Well, there are the variables to be controlled, depending on how much you talk to the child, on how much you say, "No" to them, how much you say, "Yes."

DR. B.: And how much you avoid both the "Yes" and the "No," which is also part of it.

FATHER: Yes, those are the variables . . .

DR. B.: Now, do you mean a "No" is the restraint, to your way of thinking?

FATHER: Yes. That is, it's a negative restraint.

DR. B.: All right. But isn't "Yes" a restraint too? Isn't that also a form of restraint but in the opposite direction, maybe a little more subtle?

FATHER: Well, perhaps. Because it follows the parent's wishes.

DR. B.: Of course! So you see, you exercise influence continually. Now let's get back to your child. When you asked your question you had someting very specific in mind. Why don't you ask about the specifics? You had a specific form of restraint in mind, a specific situation where you thought the child should be restrained. Otherwise you wouldn't have asked your question in the first place.

FATHER: Well, as a matter of fact, I did.

DR. B.: All right, then. Why don't you ask it?

FATHER: Oh, it's a general thing we've been thinking about and talking about, in terms of our attitude toward the child.

DR. B.: Well, don't talk about these things in general. It will only mislead you. There are no general bacteria, are there? All right, then, why don't you apply the same specificity of thinking that you've learned in your particular field to the problem of child rearing? There are no general problems in this field as there are no general problems in the field of bacteria, isn't that so? And you'd think someone very foolish if he spoke about bacteria in general, wouldn't you?

FATHER: Yes.

DR. B.: That's what I meant ... that you would never ask such a question in your own special field.

FATHER: But ... I would expect such a question from a person not in the field!

DR. B.: Oh ... well ... do you want me to expect it of you? Then, all right, I expect it of you.

FATHER: Well, I have no special questions to pose because of not being acquainted with the particulars of the field.

DR. B.: That's all right. But I can only answer in specifics.

FATHER: Well, you've pointed the way. I guess I'll have to become acquainted with the field of child rearing. In the end, it needs analysis of the problem. And that's sufficient.

DR. B.: Very good! I agree.

2

Examine Your Goals!

FATHER: I don't know if . . , this may be the start of a problem, or it might not be. We have a daughter six months old, and another child who's fifteen months. That's really close. And the baby, she's very frightened of strange people.

DR. B.: How long has she been frightened of them?

FATHER: Well, we noted it just in the last three or four weeks. And I noticed it because . . . I do know that children have a period when they become distrustful of people. But with the son, he never was, and he isn't now, distrustful. He's friendly. And while I know it's the same environment, the situation is different, because different children are treated differently. I just wondered if that's a little bit early to be distrustful, or if it isn't.

DR. B.: Yes, it is a little bit early. But if there are no other danger signs, I'd just take it to be an early-developing child.

FATHER: Well, she's a pretty sensitive child. I don't know. Sometimes she becomes pretty angry at you for nothing. Could that be another sign? I don't know. As I say, I don't even know if it's a problem. We anticipated that as soon as it got a little nicer out we'd take her out more. When the boy was only three or four months old we took him out, which we haven't done with her.

DR. B.: Why?

FATHER: Well, physically it was hard to take the two of them out. But we always have visitors.

175

MOTHER: But they're always the same visitors!

FATHER: Well, it's only been recently. She distrusts those people now, but before that she was never distrustful. And she is very sensitive, isn't she?

MOTHER: Yes.

FATHER: Sometimes if you look at her the wrong way, she gets mad. That's about what it amounts to.

DR. B.: Well, some children are more sensitive.

FATHER: Do you feel that by taking her out to a lot of places we're going to overcome her fear? Or would it only increase it? I don't know ...

DR. B.: Go on. Just go on talking. I'm listening.

FATHER: I'm about ... I was going to say, I'm about at the end of my rope, but I'm not. I've just started.

DR. B.: You haven't even started!

FATHER: But now that we are talking about it, I hate to think it's a problem. I just wonder ...

DR. B.: Well, it is a problem, but I think the problem is yours. Namely, to decide: should you expose her to strangers or shouldn't you? Do you fall in with her desire not to have visitors around? Or do you feel that that's something the child has to fight through?

MOTHER: Well, she definitely has to fight it through!

DR. B.: Why do you say that?

MOTHER: Well, I think it's important to be the kind of person that's friendly; to be an agreeable person.

DR. B.: Why is that important?

MOTHER: Well, I myself like that kind of personality.

DR. B.: All right. So what you're saying is, "I want my child to be the kind of a person that I like."

MOTHER: Yes, I guess that's about what I mean.

DR. B.: Well, if somebody were to tell you that, would you entirely subscribe that the adjustment should be hers?

MOTHER: No. When you put it that way, it doesn't sound right.

DR. B.: All right. Let's have the arguments pro and con.

FATHER: Well, you can't expect every individual to be exactly like yourself.

DR. B.: Well, now, your wife hasn't said she's that kind of person herself. All she said is that she'd like her child to be like that. So we cannot jump to conclusions. I mean, she might and she might not, but we haven't gotten any evidence as yet.

FATHER: Well, isn't the baby a bit young to worry about that?

DR. B.: I don't know. I don't say you've got to worry. I can only teach you a way of thinking. But I want you to understand very clearly: if you've acquired this way of thinking, you will run into plenty of problems. All I can do is to sensitize you to the difficulties; I cannot predict what they're going to be. Nor can I tell you how you should solve them, because I don't know. All I can help you with is not to overlook things.

Most of the children who are so seriously disturbed that they wind up at the Orthogenic School didn't get that way because their parents deliberately did things wrong. I think you'd have to look far and wide for a parent who deliberately does something to damage his child. But they overlooked things. They were unable to see, just because "it wasn't any problem."

So you see, when I want, in my own way, to help you do a better job, I try to do it by teaching you how to go about recognizing a problem, and what reasoning applies, but not by telling you what to do. Still, everybody wants to be told, because it's so easy. And then, of course, you have nobody to blame but me, which is also convenient.

[*At this point the father became silent, and another parent began to talk about getting angry with his child. It was about an hour before the father was ready to open up again, as follows.*]

FATHER: Can we start again with that problem we were talking about?

DR. B.: Sure! Basically we never left it.

FATHER: All right. Fine. I'd like to ask you a question, but I'm hesitating, because you don't like questions, and . . .

DR. B.: No, no! I never said that.

FATHER: I know. I mean, you don't like questions where you have to give an answer. I'm trying to get the answer myself.

DR. B.: Then you're on the right way, my friend.

FATHER: Speaking about getting angry with a child, I've gotten angry with my daughter . . . more so than I should have. In fact, I was very mad about it. In fact, I think I had a little bit of resentment toward her.

DR. B.: No! There you go again, not quite facing the facts. Because if you were really mad, you must have felt more than a little bit of resentment. Don't tear yourself down; you're a nice guy. If you'd felt only a little bit of resentment, you wouldn't have done anything at all. Correct?

FATHER: Well, maybe it was a lot of resentment. In thinking back, going back to why my child might be distrustful of people . . . the question I was going to ask is, what are the reasons they seem to find for children going through a distrustful period? If I knew that, then I could take some of those reasons and bring them back to what I've done. Maybe I've accelerated the step, and maybe it's not normal.

DR. B.: Look, if I were to answer that, what it would do to you would be exactly what happens to those who read the medical books: they get all the symptoms. And if I tell you the reasons why a child might become distrustful of others . . . I couldn't exhaust them, but I could offer maybe thirty. You would then be convinced that you make all thirty mistakes and you'd be gray before your age. That gets us nowhere. No! You have got to find the few reasons; I will not give you a flat number. But we get together here for the specifics—the one and only, or maybe the combination of two, or maybe three things that make your child distrustful. Do you see what I mean? If we start to find in ourselves all the symptoms and buy all the medicines for all the symptoms, we're going to kill ourselves off.

FATHER: Well, all right. Then let's continue. Could it be that one of the things is that we've neglected her more and have a little guilt complex about it? Because when she was younger, the boy was walking and he was starting to talk, and she was still in the crying, eating, sleeping stage and we didn't pay a great deal of attention to her. In fact, not even the grandparents or anybody paid her much attention at first.

DR. B.: What do you mean? You let her cry all the time?

FATHER: Oh, no! We didn't let her cry.

MOTHER: Her physical needs were attended to.

FATHER: Her physical needs were always tended to.

DR. B.: All right. For the first four months of life, if all the physical needs of the child are adequately cared for, maybe that's all the newly born infant needs; but adequately, whatever that entails.

FATHER: Then I feel that that's not the specific one, two, or three of the problem. Because all her physical needs, and possibly more than that, were taken care of. If the physical and the psychological are so closely combined ... when she was being fed she was being held. Oh, incidentally, maybe that's the reason! We don't hold her when we feed her, and we haven't for some time.

DR. B.: Why?

FATHER: Because as an infant, practically from the beginning, she didn't take a bottle well. She was too interested in what was going on. And the older she got, four, five, six weeks, the more she could see, the more she would watch you instead of eating. Also, there was a problem of having to feed two children at the same time in the morning, or close to the same time. And so we got the bottle prop—over my objections originally—but now I wouldn't give it up.

DR. B.: Why not?

FATHER: Because it's very easy.

DR. B.: For whom?

FATHER: For the parents.

MOTHER: Now, just a minute. That may be. But I've also tried very many times to hold her while I feed her, and the feeding will go on for an hour, or an hour and a half. But when I prop the bottle and there's nobody around to disturb her, she takes the bottle very nicely and very quietly. I can go in and burp her once, I go back and give her the bottle, and everything's under control. The other way she doesn't care if she eats or not. She's never been a very hungry child, and she's always been hard to feed.

FATHER: That's why I used to get mad at her. I used to get quite a temper over it.

DR. B.: Why?

FATHER: Because it was early in the morning and I didn't want her to waste my time. I'm being honest. Because the other one wanted to eat, and I thought I should get to him. I felt partial to him, or I felt a great deal partial to him. I'm not trying to disguise the reasons why. I examine them, and if it's the naked truth, it comes up.

DR. B.: Well, I think you should examine them, and I think you're doing fine. I'm still listening.

FATHER: Well, I have examined them, and they're rather naked. But I'm still trying to find out what mistakes we've made, specifically. After all, she's only six months old. And up to four months you say it's pretty much a matter of eating and sleeping. During the last two months she's gotten a lot of attention, a lot more than she did before. She's won a place in the family. Where is ... where did we fail, if we have failed? I don't know. Really, I don't know if it's a problem.

DR. B.: I don't know if it's a problem, either. All I know is that on the one hand you say, "I want my child to be nice to people, to like and enjoy company . . ."

FATHER: Her mother said that; I didn't.

DR. B.: Yes, her mother did say that. On the other hand, you say, "If I can get out of being with her, and have her feed herself all by herself, I prefer that." Do these two things jibe in your own mind, if you look at both statements? Isn't there a discrepancy, a contradiction?

MOTHER: Well, there's another fact which I think is very easily overlooked, and that is that the only thing a mother and father have to do is to take care of their children.

DR. B.: Well, I don't know. Fathers have to earn a living, too.

MOTHER: That's just it! Sometimes you need that time for something else.

DR. B.: I'm only too aware that he has to earn a living. I don't know why you're so defensive about it. Did I ever claim that the only . . .

MOTHER: Well, you said that about getting out of being with the child.

DR. B.: I didn't say that was your only wish. I said that the two wishes do not jibe. And I told you before that I cannot tell you what sort of child you should want. I can only show you whether your actions are really conducive to producing the type of child you say you want. Now, some of your own methods, it seems to me, contradict your desires; in which case your decisions don't seem reasonable.

MOTHER: Well, there's no question but that she hasn't received the same amount of attention that he did. But in a family where there are practically two babies—I mean, he's practically as much of a baby as she is, and his meals take as much time as hers—I can't

181

just give him his food and walk away from him. And it's very difficult when the meals come on at the same time.

DR. B.: Why do they have to come at the same time?

MOTHER: Well, they both have three meals a day, and she has an extra bottle. If I fed them one at eight and the other at nine and so on throughout the day, it would be meals all day long. And to be perfectly frank, I'm not the kind of person who can spend the whole day feeding people without ever having time to do anything else. I'd be very unhappy and I don't think I'd be doing my children any good.

DR. B.: So you say, "Let's face it: my children, whether they like it or not, have to be fed as I want them to be; otherwise I can't do it," which is a perfectly accurate and straightforward answer, only you didn't make it. You sounded defensive about it. So obviously you feel there's something wrong with it. I don't say there is something wrong with it; I only say that you feel there is.

If you were to say, "I'm willing to have my child suffer some, but that's the way I'm going to arrange my life and their lives, and they'd better conform to it even if they suffer," that would be a perfectly accurate and defensible statement. But in that case, you should be able to accept it that when forced to accept your ways they get distrustful of others.

MOTHER: Well, the bottle propping didn't start out that way. Once in a while I had to prop it out of necessity. It only got to be a habit after I realized that the feedings when I did prop the bottle went so much more successfully, and more milk was taken, than when I held her and fed her.

DR. B.: Why? Is the child underweight?

MOTHER: Well, my pediatrician wasn't satisfied with the amount she was taking. He certainly pushed solids. And he wanted to be sure she was taking enough.

DR. B.: All right, let me ask you. If you have nice

company and enjoy your meals, and have a good conversation at the meal, does it take shorter or longer?

FATHER: Longer.

DR. B.: Then why do you think it takes the child longer to feed from the bottle when you're with her?

MOTHER: Now, just a minute. I want to go on with this a little bit longer. He is very, very definite about a bottle feeding not taking longer than a half-hour.

DR. B.: Who?

MOTHER: My pediatrician.

DR. B.: I don't know if he has any earthly reason for that.

MOTHER: Well, that's the way he feels about it. He says that if you allow a small child to go on and on with the bottle, that it gets to be a habit. And they begin to assume that a bottle is something you play with.

DR. B.: Well, what's wrong with that? I know some pretty grown up people who still play with a bottle.

MOTHER: Well, he's the one who said it, originally.

DR. B.: Now look. If you want to obey your pediatrician's rules on child rearing, that's fine with me. But then don't ask me for advice.

MOTHER: Well, now it's too late. It's gotten past the point where I have to worry if it takes a half-hour or ten minutes. She's older than that. But this is something that started when she was a week old, or two weeks old.

DR. B.: I don't care about that. I care only about what's happening now. On the one hand, you say that you want her to enjoy company, to be cheerful. And on the other hand you tell me yourself that you eat much more cheerfully if it takes longer, and you have company. But you have just got to decide what kind of a child you want, and to take the time for it. To get the kind of child you want takes effort and plenty of time.

MOTHER: But then what happens to the other child if I allow her feeding to go on forever?

DR. B.: Does it really go on forever, or does it go on for three-quarters of an hour?

MOTHER: Oh, I imagine it's approximately that.

DR. B.: All right. Then why do you exaggerate and say forever?

MOTHER: Well, three-quarters of an hour, four times a day ...

DR. B.: Well, so what? In the day there are many hours. What else is the kid to do at the age of six months but eat? That's her only activity.

FATHER: Well, am I right in assuming, although you said the purpose of this group is not to give answers, that you're making a recommendation about feeding the child? Oh ... you're not making the recommendation? ... Okay ...

DR. B.: Examine your goals! Examine the kind of relationship you want to have with your child. And after you have definitely settled that in your mind, and your wife has settled in it in her mind, then the two of you, I think, should figure out what the differences are. And there will be differences, if you're honest with yourselves and with one another. You must settle the differences. Then you arrive at a master plan. Then you have to make up your mind whether, to get the child you have in mind, won't entail certain sacrifices on the part of you and your wife. Then you have to settle whether it's worth making such a sacrifice to get the child you want to have. And when you've done all that carefully, and have done a little soul-searching, you'll be much farther ahead in knowing what you should do than you are now. I don't say you will then have hit on the right solution, but you'll be on the way.

MOTHER: I'd like to clarify one point, though. I'm really quite satisfied with my relationship to her, and with her relationship to me. We're only concerned about her relationship to other people.

DR. B.: Well, I don't believe that a child who is regularly fed with a propped bottle will have too easy a time in establishing decent relationships to other human beings. It might be a very successful individual, you know; it might be a very intelligent individual. It need not be a bad child or a problem child, because there are many ways of life. There are people who are isolates, lone wolves, as we call them, but who otherwise are very successful citizens. You know what I mean? But social relations are established very early in infancy, and as far as we know, that's what the child enjoys most.

Now you say your pediatrician wants to prevent the forming of bad habits. Well, a person's habits, or his tendencies if you like, are established quite early in life. The tendency to enjoy one's food and to enjoy company—or to take one's food lonely and get along without company—can both be established early in childhood. But if you haven't much time or use for your child in these early months or years, don't be amazed if your child may not have much time or use for you later on, because you've started the pattern yourself.

Now I can see the way this can happen in many families. People are busy and they have little time. Well, that's all right. But then they shouldn't look for too much sociability in their child. As we know from many famous examples, very gregarious people like Churchill and Roosevelt were fed very long and very extensively; not necessarily by their mothers, but by their nurses. They turned out to be very optimistic people. They enjoyed food and drink, they enjoyed company, and they sat very long at the dinner table, chatting and having a good time.

There are other studious people who gulp their food down, lonely more or less; they aren't gregarious around the dinner table, they don't talk much, but are still successful citizens. Don't think that I'm saying that you'll make a misfit out of your child. I have no evidence for that. But there's a discrepancy between your desires for your child as you stated them, or as your wife stated them, and the way you establish certain habits in the child. Now, what you're going to do about it is entirely up to the two of you.

FATHER: Well, I feel that we're going to change.

DR. B.: Yes, but your wife feels that that might be an imposition on her time. After all, it's very easy for you—let's face it—to tell your wife to change. Then you go off in the morning and attend to your business or occupation and then come back home in the evening and expect her to have it all done. I mean, you have to see it a little bit realistically, as I was told to do. It's very easy for the husband to say, "You have got to feed her, and you have got to carry her around, and you have got to play with her for many hours each day." But then you come home and want to have a good dinner ready on time, and the house nicely cleaned, and "Why aren't my things put away," and "Do I have to work around the house as soon as I come home?" But that just doesn't go.

FATHER: Well, I feel fairly confident, now. I've examined it while we were talking, and she does get quite a lot of attention at other times, doesn't she? Her feedings are still the only times . . . they're solitary and lonely, as you say. I think we're going to change that.

DR. B.: Well, I would caution you: Don't change it overnight, because a pattern has been established. Maybe it's not a good pattern, but you have established it, and you cannot expect the child to change overnight. Do you see what I mean? Just because we had a meeting here we cannot stand the child's life on its head. Then you only add new damage to old injury.

It's true, the young child is very adaptable and very flexible. And while it might not have the best regime, it's the regime to which this organism, at a great expense of vital energy, has accustomed itself. Human beings are very flexible, and can live in the arctic or the tropics. But you shouldn't shift them back and forth without stops in between. Do you see what I mean? So don't do anything rash. Do it slowly, in slow steps.

If you now force another regime overnight, the child will resent it even more. Just add a little bit, a few minutes here and there. You go in and talk to her, or read to her, or make whatever noises you want to make. Be companionable, and increase it slowly. Even if the eating suffers a little, as it will. Don't think that she will now eat better or faster; on the contrary— because it's a new learning process. You have taught her to eat in isolation; well, she learned it. Now you want to teach her to eat in company. That again is a difficult learning process. So you have to do it in very easy steps if you want to do it at all. Does that make sense to you?

FATHER: Yes, it does.

DR. B.: That's why I'm always afraid of giving advice without really having talked it through. Because when people go home and do the exact opposite from what's become habit, the organism naturally revolts. That also goes for screaming at the child, or losing your temper. If you scream at the child all the time, it's not good for the child but he gets used to it. A sudden outburst of temper by a person who's usually gentle with a child is much harder to take, because no habits are formed for it. You see?

Don't think that you have said something positive when you say, "Most of the time I'm nice, and very rarely lose my temper ... but then I lose it." Well, it might be unavoidable, and you're a human being, and we all have our frailties and our shortcomings. But realize that with your kindness and your niceness you build up certain expectations. And whether you like it or not, you must try to live up to them.

Now! Who wants to talk next?

3

Reasoning: The Slow Way

MOTHER: I feel a little ashamed about asking you this, but last time you mentioned the cost of saying "Don't" to a child, and I don't understand what the full cost is to tell a child not to do something, or to slap him. Can you tell me?

DR. B.: Okay ... what *is* the cost? Let me say first that you'd be creating a fool's paradise if you never said, "No" or "Don't" to a child. You have to say it. What we're talking about is only a question of quantity. The question is whether it's worth expending a great deal of effort and ingenuity in order to cut down as much as we can on these "Don'ts." And it seems to me that we can reasonably accept doing something that entails hardship for us only if we understand the price that the child would otherwise have to pay.

After all, life is a long series of just such decisions and choices. In this particular case the question is: to what inconvenience will I go in order to avoid having to say, "No" or "Don't," or to slap a child, as was said here. Slapping, for example, will often bring you fast results, but it will do you no good in the long run. And why that's so we can also discuss. The reason is, very simply, that you slap your child because you're out of your wits.

MOTHER: True.

DR. B.: And the child is keenly aware of that, and it ain't good.

MOTHER: But wouldn't that be true only if you lost

your temper? I mean, couldn't you do it without anger?

DR. B.: Oh . . . how many of you—I don't want to ask how many of you slap your child—but how many of you slap a child cold-bloodedly? Can I see a show of hands? [*Two hands go up.*] Cold bloodedly? That's amazing!

SECOND MOTHER: Doctor Bettelheim, I'd like to explain that a little bit. My own child isn't slapped indiscriminately, I hope. But whenever he goes into the street, which is only about once every four months, he gets something that hurts him. It comes very determinedly and cold-bloodedly from me, and he remembers it enough in between times not to go out. He'll go up to the curb . . . and then he'll turn around.

DR. B.: Somebody's getting very excited around here. [*Turning*] Let's have it.

THIRD MOTHER: I wanted to ask her: don't you get excited if your child runs out in the middle of the street? The first thing I think is, "My God, he's going to get run over," and I grab him quick and get him away.

MOTHER: Well, you do grab him quick. You don't, well . . . just wallop him, you know? Because I've only spanked him once, but that time I was furious at him. I mean, I really was . . .

DR. B.: I know. It's always easier to be furious at him than at ourselves for lacking foresight.

MOTHER: I was furious at both of us . . .

DR. B.: And you spanked yourself, too?

MOTHER: It was worse.

THIRD MOTHER: No, but wouldn't you get excited if a child ran out in the street?

DR. B.: I don't know. I have children of my own, and at the Orthogenic School we have some forty youngsters, supposedly among the most unmanageable children in the United States; and every one of them has been taught to stay out of the street.

THIRD MOTHER: That's amazing!

DR. B.: I beg your pardon?

MOTHER: You mean you don't think that being punitive even in this one instance is justified?

DR. B.: What do you mean by being punitive?

MOTHER: Well, I mean, like she said . . . if the child runs out into the street . . . spanking him.

DR. B.: No, I don't think that's justified at all. Because then what he might say is, "All I have to do is run out into the street so that mommy doesn't see me." That's why spanking isn't a good idea as a punishment, even in this instance. All the child learns is, "I just have to make sure that mommy doesn't see me," which is very dangerous. Because then he looks for mommy instead of for the car.

I should add that if you can really explain that the danger comes from the cars, there's at least a chance that the child will look for the cars, and not for mommy who will spank. As a matter of fact many accidents happen to children in this way. They look back toward the house when they step into the street, instead of looking toward the cars. The answer is, of course, if you want to teach them not to go out in the street, and they disobey, what should the consequences be? What is the logical consequence?

FOURTH MOTHER: Remove them from the proximity of the street, that's all.

DR. B.: That's right! Since they cannot be trusted, or have not intelligence or foresight enough, or cannot control themselves well enough not to fall for temptation, they cannot be out alone. That's all there is to it. And I'm willing to teach any child to stay on the sidewalk in this way.

MOTHER: Do you think they can learn that, though? Say at fifteen or sixteen months, I mean?

DR. B.: A child of fifteen or sixteen months has no business being away from his mother's side, or his father's side.

MOTHER: Well, at what age does a usual child learn?

DR. B.: There are no usual children, my girl. But a

child of three can slowly begin to learn. Around three. Of course, some are precocious and some are slow.

FIFTH MOTHER: My little boy, when he was one and a half and was first walking, I always cold-bloodedly slapped him for crossing, and now he's just fine. He doesn't dare go in the street. And what harm has it done?

DR. B.: I don't know. Maybe none at all.

FIFTH MOTHER: I mean, could it harm him, slapping him like that?

DR. B.: Maybe not.

FIFTH MOTHER: I don't see where there's any harm.

DR. B.: I don't know; maybe none at all. Maybe everything is all right, and maybe in twenty years he will lie on the couch and pay fifteen dollars an hour to find out, "Why was my mother so harsh?"

FIFTH MOTHER: My mother slapped *me* and I haven't lain on a couch.

DR. B.: I said maybe nothing at all, didn't I?

FIFTH MOTHER: Well, it's certainly not as if I beat him.

DR. B.: Look, if you want to go on slapping, it's fine with me. I'm nobody to tell you what to do or to order you around.

FIFTH MOTHER: No, but I'd like to know what's wrong with it. I'd stop doing it if I could see something wrong with it. I'd like to see something wrong with it if it's bad.

DR. B.: It just doesn't make sense! It's an exercise of force and when the Russians do it with the Hungarians we don't like it.

FIFTH MOTHER: Oh, it isn't a whipping; it's just a little tap on the head.

DR. B.: It's still force, comparing your size and his. Sure you didn't kill him. But do you like the way things are, that this world is ruled by force and whoever's stronger beats down the weaker if he gets in his way? Then by all means let's go on slapping children.

FIFTH MOTHER: What if the mother just isn't patient enough to constantly distract the child or think up ways to get out of it? Maybe it would be better for her to train the child fast and not take any chances.

DR. B.: Are we raising objections for the mother now, or for the child?

FIFTH MOTHER: But a mother has to be considered, too.

DR. B.: Then let's stop this talk about child rearing. Let's talk about mother rearing.

FIFTH MOTHER: But if the mother gets so nervous or upset ...

DR. B.: All right. "It makes me so nervous, what the child does. It's better for the child if I'm not so nervous, so I'll hit him." How would you like such reasoning?

SECOND MOTHER: Well, I think in talking it should be considered.

DR. B.: What's the feeling of the group?

FOURTH MOTHER: Well, I've seen this. The two or three times I've spanked my older boy ... the next week or so he went around hitting all the kids in the neighborhood.

DR. B.: Of course! And then you come to me and say, "He's so unmanageable."

THIRD MOTHER: Well, I spanked my boy for hitting me. Imagine that! But he told me what sense it made to him. He said, "If you hit me, why can't I hit you?"

DR. B.: Exactly. Perfectly logical. Only he should be the one to hit you and you should be the one who doesn't hit back.

THIRD MOTHER: Why?

DR. B.: Because you should have more sense than he, and more self-control. But if you want to educate your child by force, then use anger and produce anxiety in him. I can quote you innumerable studies to show that if you want to teach something fast, you shock the person. The harder the shock or the more frequent the shock, the faster the brain will learn. And the longer the brain will remember. So there's plenty of evidence.

All the scientific evidence goes to prove that slapping or punishment, physical punishment, produces results— much faster than reasoning. Because if reasoning produced results as fast as physical punishment, the world would look much better. Reasoning is a very slow way, a very difficult process. As a matter of fact, to solve things through reasoning is the hardest way, but also the best.

MOTHER: Well, when can you really start reasoning with them?

DR. B.: When they have reason.

MOTHER: Well, that's what we're trying to find out, isn't it?

DR. B.: That's right.

MOTHER: I think it's when they can understand the "Don'ts."

DR. B.: That's right. And the question is, do you want to teach your child like a rational being or like a monkey or a trained dog? Do you want to do it by automatic responses without thinking, without reasoning, or do you want to develop his reasoning ability? If you want to develop his reasoning ability, then your punishment or your curbs must have a logical connection with the misdeed. If you want to educate him by force, obviously no. The second way has to do only with the fact that you're stronger, and with nothing else.

I am not here to tell you how to educate your children, but I just want to do away with the idea that punishment or threats are not effective means of education. They most certainly are, or they wouldn't have survived this long. But like any other means of education they have a price.

For instance, when I went to school I was taught penmanship in all the primary grades. Now, I'd say that my handwriting is, by and large, a little more legible, maybe even a little prettier, than the handwriting of the children we educate nowadays. On the other hand, I didn't get any social studies, and very little natural history. And, you know, I'm so terribly deficient in some of the natural sciences, because the time was spent on penmanship. Well, you can argue that it was more important than social studies or natural history, but the point is that everything has a price. Now to come back: what price are you willing to pay for the slaps?

MOTHER: Do you mean in time?

DR. B.: Not in time, but that you beat down the child's independence which you are later going to want to develop. You give him a demonstration that force is acceptable to you, instead of reason—that the stronger can beat the weaker one and achieve desirable results since—you think they're desirable results. If you slap him out of anger, you teach him that it's all right to be motivated by anger in reaching judgments, and so on down the line. I don't know. Then the question is, what kind of a child do you want to have? What kind of human being do you want your child to grow up to be? That, it seems to me, conditions the means of education you're going to select.

SIXTH MOTHER: Well, what's it got to do with slapping? I've only swatted my kid twice, but it was hard, and it was at five thirty, just the way everybody else does . . . at the end of the day.

DR. B.: Is it really the end of the day? Or what is it, at five thirty?

SIXTH MOTHER: It's the end of his day and the beginning of mine, to be quite frank. Then I do the housework. That's the way it runs now.

DR. B.: That's right. You did it because at that moment your housework was to you more important than doing the right thing by the child. It's so often the housework that gets the child down.

MOTHER: I've quit doing the housework.

DR. B.: Yes? Well, good for you. But not everybody can follow you there. Some mothers have to do the housework.

SIXTH MOTHER: But I mean, I don't want to hit him, and it seems to be a question of my values—what I want him to grow up to be.

DR. B.: Look, I want to make one thing very clear. We are here discussing principles, trying to learn how to think about our problems. I don't think you'll have a misfit if you slap your child once in a while.

SIXTH MOTHER: No, I know that.

DR. B.: I want to make that very clear. I know that you'll slap him once in a while anyway, whatever I say . . .

SIXTH MOTHER: Yes, well, as you just said . . .

DR. B.: Because that's human nature. We're still a little bit savage; we're not yet wholly rational human beings. But here I can only discuss a reasonable way to think about it. Whether you really want to think about it at all, and along rational lines, that's your problem.

SIXTH MOTHER: Well, what I want to know is, what's the alternative to slapping?

DR. B.: Be careful. Use forethought. And impress the child with your greater intelligence, not your size. Do you want to impress on your child that you try to think very carefully for his well-being? Or do you want to impress on him that you can beat him, hands down, in a fist fight?

MOTHER: Well, about crossing the street; they do learn it. I mean, they learn it in their play, from their friends, too. I mean . . .

DR. B.: Some do and some don't. Again, you cannot generalize. Now, I will not say that I've never lost my temper with a child, but I will say truthfully, never about such a thing as going out in the street. Or anything like it. Because there's a temptation. Other children do it. The only thing I use is, "Well, if you cannot play out in the street without stepping over the

195

curb, then you have just got to stay in." And I take the child in and I keep the child in.

Now how long—that will depend. There we have to use some reason: long enough so that I think the child will remember. But of course I wouldn't expect a child under three and a half ever to remember. Or three, let's say. You see what I mean? Or if he's bright, very bright, maybe two years and eight months. If he remembers, all to the good. And only you will know how well your own child remembers. But don't think that because he remembers most of the time he will always remember.

There's a reason why we start formalized teaching at six. Because we know that only the child of six can really learn and, after repeated experience, truly remember over a reasonable stretch of time. Those of you who have any experience with teaching will know how the first-grader forgets practically everything he's learned in reading over the summer vacation—between the first and second grades—and how reading is fully maintained over the summer only between the second and the third or fourth grades unless of course you read with the child during the summer. Well, see how fast children of this age forget even the things they've learned well?

Therefore, we really can't expect a child to learn to be careful and to always remember it, until the age when he learns to remember how to count—when he remembers his first addition facts and his first reading facts. And that's the age of six or seven. So, with safety, the logical punishment is, "If you do not know how to behave on the street, I as a responsible parent cannot let you go out alone."

Now with a small child I think you have to start to teach him when you're with him. And the first chance comes at around three. You know, the three-year-old wants to go by himself and not have to hang on to your hand all the time. Then you can say, "You may walk by yourself if you stop at the curb and wait for me." If he doesn't, then for a week don't let go of his hand, and that will be quite unpleasant for the child. As a matter of fact, it can be more disagreeable than the slap.

So you see, I'm not saying that education must be free of frustration. That's plain foolishness. Good education is often a difficult and frustrating process. But the means of education should be the logical result of what you're trying to teach, because in this way you develop first the child's intelligence and his independence, and soon his responsibility as a citizen. It isn't that I'm against the slapping because it's a painful method. I'm against it because it's a brutal and illogical method, a method based on superior force, not on superior reasoning.

4

Back-Yard Jungle

MOTHER: Dr. Bettelheim, I'm wondering if a child should be taught to stand up for himself in his own self-defense. I have a little boy who'll be starting kindergarten soon. He'll be six next week. And some of the little boys are a little larger than he is, though they're all in the same grade. But rather than fight and stick up for himself, he just stands there.

DR. B.: Well, this is an important question and I'm sorry it comes up so late tonight. But if we can't do justice to it now, we might take it up again next quarter.

My answer is, the parent must never fall down on his protective function. That is, if you tell him, "Go out and fight for yourself," you tamper with his rights; because it's his privilege to decide. If he prefers the beatings, that's his problem. Otherwise you may be putting him in a predicament he's not up to. Then he has to fight not for his own sake, because he wants to, but because you told him to. But if you leave him to his own devices, and then he comes home crying, you can say, "Here with me it's perfectly safe, and I'll be happy to have you." And in ten minutes he'll be bored and go out.

MOTHER: Then it's wrong to teach him to fight and defend himself?

DR. B.: It's not wrong, but in a way it's really none of your business. He'll learn it soon enough in this world. Now the thing is, when you're physically

198

present, then you protect your child. When you're not present, you have to offer your presence where you are. If he wants to be with his friends for the fun he has, then he must take his chances. Do you see?

MOTHER: Well, he's beginning to retire from them . . .

DR. B.: He won't retire permanently. And if so, there's not a thing you can do. That's his privilege—to become a fighter or a peaceful citizen.

MOTHER: Well, I don't approve of the fighting but I thought it was necessary . . .

DR. B.: Well . . . it depends on the age. I, personally, would never say it was good. But I think if I brought my child up in the right way he'd hit back. He won't provoke, but he'll stand for no nonsense; he'll defend himself and hit back. But there is, after all, a pecking hierarchy among children, you know? Little boys are beaten up by big boys, and so on. You just mustn't permit it when you're present, because you, as the parent, remain the source of security. You are the protector.

Out in the back yard, without you, is the jungle that reigns among children. But always be sure that the door is wide open so that he can run to you, to order and security. And if he says, "They beat me up, come out and beat them up," tell him, "No, you stay here with me. Play here." And again, sometimes you have to use a grain of salt. Because there might be a neighborhood bully, and him I wouldn't let into my yard.

SECOND MOTHER: Well, what about the younger child? Sally, my little girl, is two, and she makes no attempt to defend herself when she's being molested by the other children. So I wondered if I should tell her to hit back.

DR. B.: Why should you? It all depends on what kind of child you want to have. If you want her to be successful in the ring, then I think you should tell her to start slugging.

SECOND MOTHER: Well ... it's gotten so it's a pattern with the other children.

DR. B.: Can't she run away?

SECOND MOTHER: Well, she doesn't. She doesn't even think they're hurting her, poor thing!

DR. B.: Now look! If it hurts, she will run.

SECOND MOTHER: Yes, I think that's true. The only thing is, I don't want to teach her violence. But I feel that maybe it's the way of life and you have to learn it.

DR. B.: I don't know. The way of life is what you make it ...

MOTHER: All I know is that my husband said he had this difficulty when he was a little boy. He was kind of a sissy, and he doesn't want to have *his* little boy go through it.

DR. B.: Now look ... your husband turned out all right, or you wouldn't have married him.

MOTHER: That's true, but ...

DR. B.: Well, all right. Do you want your boy to turn out like your husband or like a prize fighter? Make up your mind.

MOTHER: Is there no in-between?

DR. B.: No! Not if you take the initiative and force it one way or the other. You see, the in-between things have to develop spontaneously. When we interfere we can only push into extremes. The in-between develops from noninterference, quite naturally. But the interesting thing is that here you say your husband was a sissy and he turns out to your liking. He was probably no sissy at all, but he may have thought he was. So obviously, being afraid of being a sissy doesn't seem such a bad idea in this culture, if it's our own fear and not that of our parents.

5

Am I a Bad Boy?

MOTHER: This isn't something that fits here, but maybe if I talk it'll become clear. We have a four-year-old, and she's asked me, "What is naughty?" Now, I'm having a hard time defining in my own mind the symbols of morality I'd like her to have.

For example, there are some things I disapprove of, and I tell her that, but I don't consider it naughty if she does them against my wishes. There are other things I can think of that obviously ... like safety rules. I say that playing with matches is naughty, and crossing the street without your mother is naughty. But beyond that she knows that I disapprove of some things, and yet I don't want her to feel that they're naughty. Naughtiness in my mind should be something forbidden, and I'm having a hard time defining it.

DR. B.: Why are naughty things forbidden? I'm sure there are plenty of naughty things that you thoroughly enjoy.

MOTHER: No ... when I say something's naughty I want it to be something that must never be done. I mean, if it's just a matter of semantics, I can use another word for it.

DR. B.: No, it's not a matter of semantics. It's not a matter of semantics at all. If you want to make your child a dumbbell, nobody can prevent you. If you want to make your child an intelligent citizen, then of course you won't throw atomic bombs and dirty hands into one basket and call them naughty. For learning you have to teach her to differentiate, don't you? Isn't that how intelligence proceeds? All right. Is there a difference between the danger of playing with matches and the danger of crossing the street, or not?

MOTHER: There isn't any.

DR. B.: There's not? I think there's a considerable difference.

MOTHER: I don't see the difference.

DR. B.: That's because you don't want your child to think. If you wanted her to think, you would try to teach her how. What would you do?

MOTHER: Teach her to cross alone?

DR. B.: No, not necessarily at her age.

SECOND MOTHER: Well, I wouldn't say the thing was naughty. I'd say that the reason she couldn't play with matches was that she might get burned, or might burn up the house, so she'd better not play with matches.

DR. B.: And why shouldn't she cross the streets alone? The reasons?

SECOND MOTHER: Oh, she might get hurt by a car.

DR. B.: That's right. But why say that it's naughty to play with matches—or to cross the street?

MOTHER: Well, it's something that I unqualifiedly don't want her to do. It's just a distinction between that, and something I disapprove of but that she can still do.

DR. B.: Such as?

MOTHER: Well, I don't approve of her getting up from the dinner table and running back and forth during dinner.

DR. B.: And what do you tell her there? What do you call that?

MOTHER: That's what I don't understand. That's what I'm trying to get the difference of.

DR. B.: Why shouldn't she get up from the dinner table?

MOTHER: It just bothers me.

DR. B.: All right, then why don't you just tell her

that? Why use the word "naughty." That's what I don't understand.

MOTHER: She doesn't ... the child doesn't know the word "naughty."

DR. B.: All right, let's start again. Your girl asks you what is naughty. Why does she ask it?

MOTHER: Because she wants to get it clear in her mind, I think, the difference between what is absolutely forbidden and what is just disapproved of.

DR. B.: But why should she use the word "naughty" for it?

MOTHER: Oh, I use it.

DR. B.: Yes, I was convinced of that.

MOTHER: Oh, but I've just used it in regard to safety rules.

DR. B.: But why are safety rules naughty? That's not even common English usage.

MOTHER: Well, this is what I want to get clear ... I mean ... I know why I used that ...

DR. B.: Yes, but I think you confuse the poor child. If you want your child to be a reasonable citizen then you have to give, for each of your actions, the specific reasons, because that's how intelligence develops. It develops by exploring the specific attributes of a specific situation, and you deny the child this right to explore if you use one global word for entirely different things. If you keep on this way you'll get an automaton who divides activities into those that are fully naughty, partly naughty, or not naughty. But you cannot have an intelligent citizen and tell the child it's naughty to cross the street, because it's not—because you do it yourself all the time.

MOTHER: Well, would it have made any difference if I said "bad"? Naughty is synonymous with bad, isn't it?

DR. B.: No, it isn't. Besides, I certainly don't think that crossing the street is bad.

MOTHER: Well, how else do you convey a generalization to a child, unless you ...

DR. B.: Isn't "dangerous" as good a generalization as "naughty"?

MOTHER: Yes, I think it is.

DR. B.: But dangerous—what does dangerous imply? What question?

MOTHER: Well, some vague . . .

DR. B.: No, what does dangerous imply?

MOTHER: Well, "Why?"

DR. B.: Yes, "Why is it dangerous?" And you can then demonstrate . . . and tell her why it's dangerous. And she will quickly see that each action is dangerous in a different way. Correct? All right. Isn't that how thinking proceeds? Don't you want your child to be able to figure out why an action is dangerous? With your term "naughty" you prevent that.

MOTHER: Yes, but I did think that as the child got older I'd explain more. After all, you've got to be adamant about certain things as long as possible.

DR. B.: Oh, I certainly don't say you've been wrong in being adamant about safety rules. Not because they're naughty, but because it's dangerous to transgress them. But I don't think I'd want my child to think it's dangerous to cross the street because she might be burned to death. Now, that's silly, but that's the connection you establish in the child's mind. And if you want an intelligent child you have to go to the trouble of explaining each thing on its own merits, not by using global terms like "naughty." Does that answer your question?

MOTHER: Yes.

THIRD MOTHER: That raises another point. We don't use the word "naughty" or "bad" or "good," but Paul's picked them up in nursery school. And now he wants to know what's "bad" and what's "good." He's been called a bad boy, and of course we assure him he's not.

DR. B.: Well, just tell him not to give you that stuff. When he comes home and says, "Johnny's bad," I'd say, "Don't give me that stuff. Tell me what you don't like about Johnny!"

THIRD MOTHER: Oh, I see. Well, what if he says that somebody called him a bad boy, and we assure him he isn't? What do you do?

DR. B.: I would ask, "Are you?"

THIRD MOTHER: We have asked him that. And he says that so and so said it.

DR. B.: Oh, all right. "I'm not interested that so and so said that."

SECOND MOTHER: After we scold Bobby now, he says, "Am I naughty?" And you never know what to answer.

DR. B.: No. But it's very interesting. These things they don't learn by themselves. You call them that once or twice, and other people have called them that, and then we're in a mess. It's not a tragic mess, you understand. But it's a mess. Because this business of whether one is nice or not comes up after a scolding. After one has done something bad, then mommy says, "But you're a nice boy," and you undo it and wipe it all out. You might as well not go to the trouble of scolding.

SECOND MOTHER: You wouldn't fall for that?

DR. B.: I wouldn't fall for that at all. I wouldn't let the discussion deteriorate to such a low level! You see what I mean? I'd say, "Now look, my boy . . ." How old is your boy?

SECOND MOTHER: He's three. Almost three.

DR. B.: Well, at three it depends on the verbal level. At four they can talk a little better. But these patterns are established very early, when talking to them is still very difficult. That's why we fall for such nonsense in the first place.

SECOND MOTHER: Yes, I see that.

DR. B.: The real difficulty is the strain of explaining to a three-year-old what is dangerous, and why it has to be avoided, and all that. Bringing it down to a language they can understand isn't easy, and that's why we fall for this kind of silly global term, and then we never get out of it. Because then a frame of mind is already created in the child which doesn't encourage investigation. Because to the child, too, it's so much simpler to ask, "Is it naughty?" instead of trying to figure it out for himself. So we're right back to the problem of freedom.

Sure, it's easier for the child to say, "Oh, that's naughty, I can't do that," instead of trying to figure out and understand, to watch and explore. Now, in your case I'd say, "Now look, I'm not interested in that business. Do you understand what happened? Do you understand why you made me angry?" And then I would very slowly and very carefully—but not too long, you know, in two or three sentences—go over the whole business. And when it's all over I would say, "Do you understand?" But I wouldn't let myself be involved in "Am I a nice boy? Was I a bad boy?"

MOTHER: Well, what kind of words do you use to distinguish? If you don't use "good" and "bad" and "nice"?

DR. B.: Why try to put everything on a moral level, whcih is very difficult for a child to understand? The child isn't interested in whether it's good or bad; he's interested in whether he's liked or not liked. Those are emotions he can understand. And you like him because he's your child, and not because he's nice. Correct?

The issue, "Am I a nice boy? Am I not a nice boy?" is an issue I wouldn't permit to arise. "You are Johnny and you're fine with me, but sometimes you do things I don't like you to do, and that was one of them. Do you understand why I didn't like that. All right, if you understand, that's all I'm interested in. So go; run along, my boy." But of course if you tell him, "Nice boy, good boy," you know, and "Isn't he a nice child?" then of course you never get away from it. Then, whether he's good or bad depends on your, or Uncle

Joe's judgment, and that's something I wouldn't wish on a dog—that somebody else's judgment should establish the worth or the worthlessness of a person. I think that he alone is the one to judge if he's a nice person or not. But I wouldn't even give him those words. It's a miserable way to think of a child, anyway.

He *is*. Period. "Am I nice?" "Well, there's a divided opinion on that." "Okay, who wins now? Shall we take a vote?" Don't you see on what an impossible basis you then establish the self-feeling, or the poor self-opinion of an individual? If you did you would immediately say, "Oh, I'm not interested. I just want him to feel good." Well ... it's not that I think these are central issues, you understand. But since you bring them up I'm discussing them.

SECOND MOTHER: We ... there are some things I've been saying, "Good" to him about.

DR. B.: Such as?

SECOND MOTHER: Oh, going to the toilet and doing a "good" job. Sometimes when things aren't going so right I say, "Maybe you'll do better tomorrow." Does that keep it out of the generalized talk?

DR. B.: Oh, I wouldn't hesitate at all if a child brings me a drawing, to say, "That's very nice," if I think it's nice. Do you see what I mean? Because the child brings you something to be evaluated. If I don't think it's nice, I don't say it. But if the child insists I say, "Well, you've made better drawings. This one I don't like so much."

SECOND MOTHER: You mean you just talk about one thing at a time.

DR. B.: That's right. And I don't think you have to approve of everything a child does, but you have to approve of the child. The very idea that we talk to the child as if we questioned his entire goodness or badness is very obnoxious to me and that's why I spend time on this discussion. I think that as parents we have the right to judge every single action if we keep it strictly on

207

that level. But we must never arrogate to ourselves the right to sit in judgment on the child in totality.

This is a principle that I think is very important. If you keep things on the level of the specific incident, you can afford to be quite strongly disapproving of a particular action. If my child aggravates me by running back and forth from the table, I would say, "Now look, if you leave the table, then you stay away. But this getting up and down . . . no! Either you stay with us or whenever you're tired you may leave us." And I would establish it well and say, "No, I will not let you do that." But it has nothing to do with whether he's a good or a bad child.

MOTHER: But is it a good or bad thing? Every action can be put in those terms.

DR. B.: But why should they be? Then you have continuously to sit and judge things.

MOTHER: But I think that every mother does, even if they don't realize it. Whether they say, "Fine job," or "Nice work," or "Good," or any sort of word, they're creating that feeling in the child.

DR. B.: Correct. But the question is: do you present the pattern to the child, or do you give him the pieces and let him put the pattern together himself? Do you, in the final analysis, give the job to the child, or do you do the job for him? The child's feeling of being liked, of being a good individual, depends on the material you present him with. But there's still a great difference in the designs, depending on whether you present the ingredients—you, and his teacher, and his friends—or whether you sit in judgment on the whole of him. And I don't think that any human being has the right to evaluate another human being—not even a mother with her child. I think we have the right to evaluate specific actions but not the total person.

MOTHER: But the child himself will evaluate himself from the specifics, will he not?

DR. B.: Correct. And that we can counteract, if need be.

MOTHER: Well, how do you do that?

DR. B.: When the child comes and says, "Am I a bad child," I would say, "Certainly not. But I didn't like what you were doing."

MOTHER: And you think a child will understand the difference when you say, "You're not a bad child, but I didn't like what you were doing"?

DR.B.: If you do it long enough, are persistent enough, and don't undo it, yes. It will ... yes, he will.

MOTHER: Oh, well, that's what I couldn't quite believe. That a child will understand the difference.

DR. B.: He will, sooner or later ... not the first time. But as a matter of fact, that's why the child will question you. As your child questions you, "Am I a nice boy?" "Am I a good girl?" he's wondering, "Because I just did something bad does it mean that I'm bad?" And if you say, "No, you're a nice boy, really," this one action decides it. So I'd be quite insistent: "I don't want apologies, or anything of the like. It's all over with, there's no need to apologize. But I didn't like what you did." "Do you like me?" "Of course I like you, but I didn't like what you did."

And about what I disapprove of I would be quite direct and outspoken. And when the child understands, I would drop the subject. If you really like your child, I don't think you have to fend for him if he does something wrong. I think you have to be honest with him. And I don't see why a three-year-old shouldn't understand that. In this way you divorce the individual from the act.

Particularly with a child, we know that because he cannot always comprehend or control his desires he'll do innumerable things that he shouldn't, in our eyes. Therefore we have the even greater task of showing him that it's these things he did, and not him, that we disapprove of. That's why I would never say, "It was

209

bad that you crossed the street." I would say, "It's a terribly dangerous thing to do, but it isn't bad. It is lacking judgment." And I would go through the discussion repeatedly.

If the child doesn't stay on the sidewalk and you feel he shouldn't go out alone, or cross the street, I would say, "No, I'm sorry! You're not old enough to walk by yourself. Therefore I will hold your hand," as we just recently discussed. But that has nothing to do with good and bad. You see, what you tried to do was to establish an iron rule, so that you wouldn't have to watch. But your obligation as a mother is to watch. Therefore, if the child steps out in the street, I would grab him if he doesn't stop. I would be very consistent and not fall for any arguing or promises.

He will cry out, "I won't do it again, I won't do it again," but I'd say, "Nothing doing. You have shown me that you did it, and you're just too young to go by yourself. So you will hold on to Mommy's hand." And after two or three weeks, I would try it again. But that doesn't make the child good or bad, or naughty or not naughty. "It's dangerous, and I don't want you to get hurt. But if you step out beyond the sidewalk, I will certainly hold your hand, and that's all there is to it. If you want to walk by yourself, all you have to do is stay on the sidewalk."

That makes sense. And believe me, the three-year-old can understand it . . . if you do it consistently enough . . . and long enough and without getting angry and excited; because if you do, then he's so full of his reaction to your anger or excitement that he can't listen to your reasoning, or understand it.

6

Is It a Good World?

MOTHER: I want to know ... if a child is learning to walk, and she bumps herself and cries, to what extent do you comfort her then?

DR. B.: Absolutely, and as much as she wants. After all, you don't want her to give up walking.

MOTHER: In other words, when they do bump, or she bumps her head against the play pen, I should go ahead and comfort her.

DR. B.: Of course. Otherwise only the double damage is done. The bump was received and no comfort came. Always comfort your child when she screams, or gets hurt. But sometimes, you know, you must be realistic. Because sometimes it's very important that they don't start to use that as a weapon over you.

MOTHER: Well, I was beginning to wonder about that.

DR. B.: That's okay. How old is the child?

MOTHER: She'll be a year old next month.

DR. B.: Well, there you can't do much. Later on you may want to say very definitely, "There's nothing wrong with you," but still comfort her. But let me make it very clear—the child shouldn't be able to fool you. If she hasn't hurt herself but comes wailing to you, you can say, "You haven't hurt yourself at all, but let me comfort you anyway. Come. Come now and sit in my lap and stay with mommy," or however you talk to your child.

MOTHER: What about putting fingers into places

where she can obviously get them out and saying, "eh-eh" till I come and see? Should I say, "I know you can get them out yourself, but I'll help you?"

DR. B.: That's right. "I know you can do it yourself. You just want mommy to come." Just tell them that, so that they don't think they've found a way to fool you. Because then you're sunk and they'll do it several times a day. Do you see what I mean? There is something moral in the child, so just tell her, "All right, you want the comfort? Here, have it; it's yours." Because very often it's nothing but the child's testing of whether the comfort is always available. And if she knows it is, it'll give her an awful lot of security. But this security is lost if she thinks she's fooling you. Only, with a one-year-old you cannot do that yet.

MOTHER: Well, I was wondering. You'd mentioned to someone with an older child that it wasn't wise to avoid their glance when you found them reaching for a forbidden object and you didn't want to raise a fuss at the moment. [*Turning*] Wasn't that when your child reached for an ash tray? Well, our child—when she bangs her head, and when she sits down a little harder than she expected, never hurting herself very badly, but bumping herself or jarring herself—she always looks up first. And if no one's around and she's in a room by herself, she just goes her own way. But if she looks first, and if someone's looking at her, she cries, and I've found myself looking the other way. Yet if it's serious, she'll cry and I'll go to her. Now, what is she asking for, in looking around?

DR. B.: Well, the thing is, "Is it a good world or a bad world? I bump myself, so it's a bad world. But if mommy's nice to me, then it's still a good world." She's trying to find out what kind of a world it is.

MOTHER: Well, why doesn't she think of finding out when no one's looking at her?

DR. B.: Because, after all, if she's bumped herself and no one knows it, who can make the world nice for her?

MOTHER: Well, I should think she'd realize that even if she's in the other room, if she'd let us know, we'd come.

DR. B.: Ah! That's something different! You agree that there's a difference, which is very true. If the child has really hurt herself badly, she will scream whether the mother is present or not. Then it's a clear-cut issue. This is a bad world! But a child who bumps herself and looks is a child who wonders, "Now is it a bad world or a good world?" Do you see what I mean?

MOTHER: Yes. She's not so badly hurt that she has to go looking for it, and all she wants is, "You're not badly hurt, but come here."

DR. B.: That's right. It's this little bit of comfort, you know. "Now, it's all right. It wasn't so bad."

MOTHER: Well, next time I'll comfort her. Before, I'd always swing around in the other direction.

DR. B.: Why?

MOTHER: It takes time to go over and give her a little pat. It happens very frequently, and it gets to the point where you think it won't happen next week, probably.

DR. B.: Oh, no. It will, it will. But do you understand the principle? That is, if you're badly hurt, then it's a bad world and we wail. We bewail our fate. But there are some small hurts that make us dubious, and that's where the comforting really counts. Because if the child is badly hurt, then the comforting really doesn't count. It doesn't make it a good world, it just makes it not such a bad world. But really meaningful, really important for the child's outlook on life, and his security, is the other—when the child is dubious. Then you can do something extra to make the child comfortable.

SECOND MOTHER: Well, no matter how long we play with our youngster, the minute we put him down, he begins to howl.

DR. B.: Do you understand what he wants?

213

SECOND MOTHER: He wants us to keep on playing with him.

DR. B.: Of course.

SECOND MOTHER: And I don't know how to console him on that.

DR. B.: There is no consolation. The world is just not as good as he wants it to be. But you realize that with each of these steps it makes the world seem less good than it could appear. Now, there are limitations to what you can do. After all, you're a human being, you get tired and all that's taken for granted. But always realize that the optimism and pessimism, the courage with which we face life, or the defeatist attitude which makes us avoid life, is established at this early age. And it's very, very difficult to change that later on. It takes years and years of hard work, if we achieve it at all.

The more you give the child the impression that this is a good world, the happier the child will be, the more courage he'll have to face the world with, because he's convinced that basically it's a good world. The less you give, the more defeatist his attitude will be, the more his conviction will be that it's a bad world anyway, and what's the use of trying. Now, you as a parent will have to choose. What sort of outlook do you want your child to have? I know there are limitations to what we can do, but . . .

SECOND MOTHER: Well . . . it's so . . . it's every time! You'd think that sometimes he'd be satisfied.

DR. B.: Why should he? How old?

SECOND MOTHER: One year old.

DR. B.: What stimulation does the world hold for a one-year-old? After all, there's very little stimulation for them besides what the mother, or the father, or maybe an older sibling provides. They're quite alive but they cannot really do very much. I mean—toys, and the playpen, and the crib. What else?

SECOND MOTHER: Toys, and a room—or the crib, or playpen, or mommy or daddy's lap.

DR. B.: Sure. This is just a difficult age, the age of the toddler. The difficulties begin there. They fall all the time, they hurt themselves, their coordination is poor, their desire is to get around and play. These are the critical ages, from one to three. But what you do to help does a lot to shape the future. They're awfully small, the beginnings, but that's where the future begins.

7

Can You Love Too Much?

MOTHER: I have an off-shoot to that . . . about re-straining a child.[1] Where should a person draw the line on the amount of love a child gets at home, as opposed to how much resistance to this . . . the affection he's not going to get when he's not at home any more? Is it possible to love a child too much?

DR. B.: Just a moment. I think you have a very important question, but I'm sorry to say, my girl, that it came out a little bit confused.

MOTHER: I'm sure it did.

DR. B.: All right, can you try it again?

MOTHER: Okay. Is it possible to love a child too much at home?

DR. B.: Is it possible for your husband to love you too much?

MOTHER: No!

DR. B.: It also takes place in the home, I hope?

MOTHER: But . . . he's not going to get that much approval outside . . .

DR. B.: Well, you see, since you're a lady, I won't be as hard on you as I was on this gentleman. Because he's a scientist and should have a scientist's training.

1. Originally this interchange followed the one titled "Cause and Consequence" in which a father raised the question of how much restraint to impose on a child.

But what do you mean by "love"? When I ask you, can your husband love you too much, it all depends on what you call love. I think we all recognize that a lot of restraint, and suppression, and brow-beating can go under the cloak of love. Underneath can hide jealousy, or possessiveness, or what have you. Now that kind of love is too much, but it isn't love in the first place. Maybe lots of parents love their children too much, but actually what's too much is their possessiveness. The desire to run the life of another isn't love.

MOTHER: Yes, I'm aware of that part of it . . . but what I mean is a certain amount of gentleness, and a certain amount of cuddling and approval. I find it very easy to give a great deal of approval, and I'm wondering if that's not too much.

DR. B.: What?

MOTHER: Well, no one else is going to approve of him as much as I do.

SECOND MOTHER: All the more reason for you to do it.

MOTHER: Yes, but isn't it going to be a jolt to the child when he finds out that nobody else is going to do it as much?

SECOND MOTHER: No, not if the parents do it.

DR. B.: Well! Go ahead . . . go ahead. Finally I start to harvest results from my labors.

SECOND MOTHER: I think it's very much easier to take this from the outside world if you know that at least somebody you like is approving of you.

MOTHER: Yes, but suppose he goes on the sidewalk and somebody snatches something away from him. Won't he feel sort of sat down on?

SECOND MOTHER: Yes, but he'll feel much worse if you sit on him too. *Then* what's he got?

MOTHER: I know, but . . .

DR. B.: Could you possibly tell me why you need me at these meetings?

SECOND MOTHER: [*slowly*] Well . . . I'm getting to

217

the point where all I have to consider is that I'm going to ask you a question, and I immediately know the answer!

DR. B.: That's right! Because the answer is obvious once you've learned how to analyze the problem—that is, to ask the right questions. Well, that's very nice. Go ahead, the two of you.

THIRD MOTHER: Well . . . I . . .

DR. B.: No, she still has the floor.

MOTHER: Well, no. I don't . . . I want to know what somebody else . . .

DR. B.: No, no! This is a very important problem and I'm not satisfied. I think she gave you the right answer, but I think you're not ready to accept it.

MOTHER: Well, I've always believed in giving him . . .

DR. B.: Yes, but your belief is not enough. The inner conviction is still lacking, and I can see it by the way you answer.

THIRD MOTHER: Maybe she can consider it in the same way as her husband's feelings toward her . . . that he loves her more than anybody else in the world.

DR. B.: How do you know?

MOTHER: Well, I don't know . . .

THIRD MOTHER: But he does have a very great affection for her . . .

DR. B.: How do you know?

FOURTH MOTHER: I think it would help if she could think of the child in terms of . . . say, a young sapling. I always feel that the more sun and the more light and rain a young sapling gets, the better it can withstand the battering of the storm it will get later on. And I think that this thinking can be applied to the child. That the more nurturing, the more . . .

DR. B.: Yes, but why do you need a sapling for that? A child will do nicely.

FOURTH MOTHER: Well, I was trying to draw an analogy.

218

DR. B.: Yes, but you can get caught in that analogy. There's a great deal to what you say, but there's still a hitch. And it goes back to the initial question of what do you want. There's no doubt that the child who's been buffeted around a great deal will develop certain defenses; they will desensitize him to a certain degree. Given enough disappointments, people who've been pushed around very badly may develop very sick defenses. Sometimes it's called armoring, because it really has the function of an armor.

That's a term used by Wilhelm Reich many years back. He spoke of an armored body and an armored soul. And you can armor yourself, or life can force you to build such an armor. But firstly, such a lot of energy goes into building such an armor. And secondly, it doesn't allow you free movement. Last of all, it armors you against the good things as well as the bad, which is the vicious thing about armor. You develop it to protect yourself from bad effects. But it protects you equally from the good influences, or I should say, it prevents them from reaching you. And that has something to do with the human psyche.

One of the great problems of education is the need to develop an armor against the bad things without also blocking out the good things. But for that we must wait. Obviously the human psyche is not yet able to develop that. Now, if you thought that basically this was such a bad world, that so few good things are done in this world that one is better off with a heavy armor, then your reaction would be very different. But you needn't worry. Because if you thought this a miserable world, your child would develop an armor anyway.

MOTHER: You mean I could make a tough guy out of him just by thinking he should be a tough guy.

DR. B.: Yes ... and that you've got to be tough to get along.

MOTHER: But he's not a tough guy.

DR. B.: Well, do you want him to be a tough guy?

MOTHER: No!

DR. B.: Then you're preventing him from becoming one. Do you see how this reaches everywhere? It's very fancy, but, in fact, we have no real freedom. Because if we're convinced that this is a miserable world and we have to be tough in it, this very conviction will be transmitted to the child, and reinforced by the way we educate him to be tough in this world.

MOTHER: Well ... then maybe I'm making him too soft.

DR. B.: Now that's a problem. Do you make him too soft? Do you make him too gentle?

MOTHER: Well, his father's gentle. And he's gentle, too.

DR. B.: Then obviously you like gentle people.

MOTHER: Yes, but isn't it bad for him to be gentle? Isn't he going to be hurt too much?

DR. B.: Would you rather be tough, or would you rather be gentle?

MOTHER: Gentle ...

DR. B.: But you know that you're going to be hurt on occasion by being gentle.

MOTHER: Don't tough people also get hurt on occasion?

THIRD MOTHER: But they have armor.

DR. B.: So you're convinced that it's better to be gentle. Why do you still argue with me?

MOTHER: Well, I just wondered. Because every once in a while I worry that maybe I'm making it too wonderful for him at home.

DR. B.: How old is he?

MOTHER: He's two and a half.

[*Burst of laughter from the group*]

DR. B.: Well, it's a problem. But I think ... it's true that the child can be spoiled by being given in to when he should learn to master a situation, but I say that with great hesitation. In general I think the error is toward toughness in our society. But this is a very nice group and I think I might for once consider the opposite. I think that if a child has had a very bad experience, but one that I consider part of the normal course of events, I would comfort the child.

But I would say clearly—and at two and a half you can already talk this way—I would say, "Well, that's the way ... that's what can happen to you. That's how life is." "It's unpleasant to be sick, but sometimes people are sick, you know." "Well, if you run, you might fall down and hurt yourself." And be very sorry that he fell, and you pet him, or whatever you do when he falls. But your statement should establish the objectivity of the situation, and also that though he fell, he cannot give up walking or even running when he feels like it.

MOTHER: To accept it and go on.

DR. B.: Yes. "This is part of living. If you want to live, you have to take some buffeting. But I will comfort you, because I love you." Do you now see what I mean?

MOTHER: Yes.

DR. B.: I will not say, "You have to take it and not cry ... because it's going to happen." I tell him, "Crying is all right and being unhappy is all right. But don't fool yourself, its going to happen to you again. Because that's life." Because in this way you can be quite realistic and avoid the spoiling. Yet I don't think you did that in the first place ... or did you?

MOTHER: Well ... not too much.

DR. B.: Sure ... he'll have some nasty companions in school, and some unpleasant teachers, and some other unpleasant experiences. But I'd be quite realistic. I would comfort him and say, "Yes, there are also bad things in this world. This world isn't perfect, and you ain't perfect either, my child." And I'd say, "But there are also many good things, and the best of them is that

221

the two of us are in it together." But this last you had better not say. Just show it through your actions. Does that answer your question? But don't say, "Yes" if it doesn't.

MOTHER: Yes, it does.

V

Battle Fatigue

From the preceding conversation it appeared that many mothers had learned to ask the right questions. They had also learned that by thinking about themselves and the child, and then by talking with him, they could usually find reasonable solutions. This willingness of the parent to take the problems of daily living seriously is the real key to the relations between parent and child. Firstly, it provides the experience that all important problems of living together as a family can be mastered if we seriously try. And secondly, this experience is what children need most—much more than being handled correctly, though the latter helps, too.

Up to now, almost all problems were presented as those of the child to start out with, though they often turned out to be parental problems too. Still, the starting assumption was that these problems originated with the children. But in any twosome, the problem of relations can originate with either partner. And even problems that are strictly the parents', particularly the mother's, when unrecognized or unresolved soon begin to affect the child and eventually the entire family. This last chapter is therefore devoted to discussions that centered clearly on problems of the mother.

Among them one dominates: the tremendous task of adjusting to domestic life after the first child arrives. In times past and in other societies, the girl's life before marriage was one long preparation for just such a life, and after marriage she met these tasks on her own. Not so in our society; certainly not so for this group of mothers; and more and more women seem to be finding themselves in the same boat. Much as all of them have looked forward to marriage and children, life has prepared them quite otherwise. In high school their course work was much the same as that of career-oriented boys; and the preparation was even less differentiated from the man's for those women who went on to college. When they did marry, they sometimes kept on with college, more often with holding a job that supported the two of them while the husband completed his schooling. So even marriage did not prepare them for domestic life, since the running of the household took second or third place after studies and/or work.

This situation changes rather suddenly when the first child is born. True, the mother usually stopped working during the last stages of pregnancy, but that in itself was a novelty; and for the rest, the pregnancy commanded all her remaining energy and interest. After that came childbirth and a few weeks of recovery and adjustment to the baby. But once this was over, it suddenly hit her that she was now to live a life very different from the one she had known.

In the incidents that follow, four mothers are confronted with their resultant restlessness and dissatisfaction with life, at varying stages of understanding, or fighting to understand the reasons behind it. In each case it is relatively clear how the actual or potential impact on the child becomes less, or fades away entirely, as the mother comes closer to understanding. The problem, though conditioned by her place in society, reveals itself to be really hers alone, or perhaps her's and her husband's, but it is not yet truly a problem of the child's.

1

This Beautiful Life

MOTHER: I have a boy eight months old. He's our only child ...

DR. B.: And you have no problems?

MOTHER: Well, everytime I come here, I mean to ask a question but I never get around to asking it. Then, today I thought I would ask you what to do. During the last three days he's started to stand up, to pull himself up to a standing position, and his whole personality seems to have changed.

DR. B.: The world looks very different.

MOTHER: Well, but he just vocalizes from morning to night. He isn't moving or active, he's just making these sounds and he seems in a state of euphoria. But after a while, it affects me just the way his crying does. It sounds like too much!

[*A burst of laughter*]

DR. B.: What else makes you think it's too much?

MOTHER: It just never stops! It just keeps on all day for twenty-four hours!

DR. B.: Now, just a moment! Twenty-four hours a day?

MOTHER: All day long he's ...

DR. B.: Now, just a moment!

MOTHER: Well, during the latter part of the day he gets more active ... physically. Then he isn't vocalizing quite as much, or in the same way. When he's moving or standing up, he makes more aggressive sounds, more of a noise like "Baa-aa, baa-aa, baa-aa!"

[*Another burst of laughter*]

DR. B.: Why do you say aggressive?

MOTHER: Well, they ... he looks that way. When he stands up he looks as if ... well, as if he were angry; that it was such a struggle to get up there, and ...

DR. B.: Yes, it's quite possible. It was probably a great struggle.

MOTHER: But before that, you see, his tones were sweet, happy sounds. And so were his noises.

DR. B.: He hadn't met up with the serious problems of life!

MOTHER: Well, he's always vocalized a great deal.

DR. B.: Yes?

MOTHER: And now he just never seems to stop.

DR. B.: Don't worry about it; he will.

MOTHER: But I ... well, that's it, you see. I don't know whether it's tension, or ...

DR. B.: Tension? What do you mean by tension?

MOTHER: Well, *I* feel it, so I wonder if he feels it!

DR. B.: Ah-h! Now you're talking. But you're talking about yourself!

MOTHER: Maybe that's it. It's really very difficult. By the end of the day he's really very irritated from his struggles.

DR. B.: Of course. That's understandable.

MOTHER: And then by the end of the day he begins to whine and cry.

DR. B.: Well, I'm really more perturbed by your own tension, and your interpreting his sounds as aggressive. After all, standing up is a great achievement!

MOTHER: Well, it was the first day he could stand up. It was also the first day that he grabbed the bottle out of my hand all of a sudden. He's always taken the spoon out of my hand when I feed him; he plays with

229

it, stirs with it. But now he grabs it like he does the bottle, and it was the first time he cried when I took something out of his hand. He just raged so hard that he couldn't even see when I was trying to put it in his other hand. These were all things that he went through pretty amiably before. And it all changed in one day.

DR. B.: Well, sometimes it happens fast. Do you have reason to think there was something special about this day?

MOTHER: No. That's what I mean . . . that I don't really have a problem. But I do get sort of tired of this "beautiful life"! [*A great deal of laughter*] It hasn't been since he used to cry all the time that I've had this feeling that I wish he'd stop!

DR. B.: Now look, how long does he really keep it up?

MOTHER: Well, I suppose I really should watch the clock. But it does seem as if it's from the time he wakes up in the morning until late afternoon.

DR. B.: Without interruption?

MOTHER: Except for his naps.

DR. B.: And while he's eating?

MOTHER: No, he's quiet then.

DR. B.: And I could probably find other interruptions if I just knew what to ask! So, it isn't really from morning to night; it just seems so to you. Well, there's no doubt about it; you're perturbed about something. Maybe it's without reason; I don't know. Probably you have very good reasons for being perturbed but I'm afraid I don't know them.

MOTHER: I suppose I'm anticipating the difficult period, now that he's being more energetic and able to move around. I guess I just didn't expect it to happen so soon.

DR. B.: Did you expect him to be around the house for the next eighty years?

MOTHER: Oh, no, no. But at least it should have been more gradual. Also I do wonder about keeping him entertained during that time so he doesn't get quite so irritated during the afternoon.

DR. B.: How do you entertain him?

MOTHER: Well, that's it. I wonder if there isn't something I can do.

DR. B.: What are you doing for him now?

MOTHER: Well, I walk him more in the buggy, for one thing.

DR. B.: And does he cry all that time?

MOTHER: No.

DR. B.: All right! That's another interruption!

MOTHER: Well, in the late afternoon I spend more time outside with him.

DR. B.: Couldn't you go out and do your shopping in the morning?

MOTHER: Well, he's just singing then. It's just later on that he . . .

DR. B.: Now look, when does he make this aggressive "Baa-aa, baa-aa, baa-aa"?

MOTHER: It's just in the afternoon, when he's struggling to do things.

DR. B.: Okay. Let him struggle a little, let him struggle.

MOTHER: And let him cry?

DR. B.: That I don't know. I'm not convinced that his crying is really as aggressive as you think.

MOTHER: Oh, no, the crying is plain irritation at not being able to . . .

DR. B.: So when is he aggressive?

MOTHER: When he tries . . . well, for instance, he has one of these teeter-chairs, and all he does with it, instead of rocking or anything . . . he sort of stands up and shouts. He just stands up.

DR. B.: Well, it's a tremendous achievement! I don't think ever in our lives will we know an achievement compared to this one. Naturally he gets excited! The question is, why do *you* get excited about it?

MOTHER: I guess it just bothers me. And if he

reaches for something . . . he has a ball that he reaches for and it rolls away, and he cries. But before this, if such a thing happened he'd just roll over and sing.

DR. B.: Because now he knows what he wants, and he wants it. Before that he didn't know, so he didn't care. Why should that upset you so much?

MOTHER: Well, yes. He's getting smarter now. It has to be expected. But it doesn't disturb *him*.

DR. B.: I don't know. What I'm afraid is that if it continues to disturb you, it might disturb him. Right now his attention is very short. His curiosity is easily stimulated and easily satisfied, as you know. And I think these toys that move away and you can't really hold on to are rather frustrating. So I'd say, let's leave it now and see where we stand in three weeks, yes?

In the meantime, try not to interpret it as aggressiveness. Don't interpret it as "too much" if you possibly can. Just take it in your stride. And always realize these are small problems. Try to see his efforts as signs of independence. And while just now there's more sign than independence, pretty soon there'll be some true independence, things he'll really be able to handle on his own. Which means that slowly there'll be less and less demands on your time and your energies.

For this mother, several issues converged to make her irritated and anxious, though the discussion was fragmentary and the issues do not stand out too clearly. Still, it is a good example of how a perfectly natural anxiety in the mother can make life with her child difficult and disappointing. I am talking about the mother's fears, particularly with her first child, about whether she will prove to be a good mother or not.

As long as her infant is by and large satisfied, life with him and the continuous care he demands may be tiring and even boring at times, but the worst this may mean is that having an infant is less exciting and more work than she expected. The disappointment still does not threaten her hopes of being successful as a mother.

But when the child begins striving to achieve and then bewails his inadequacies—a perfectly natural development—his exasperated crying may feed into his mother's anxiety about herself. Then each new cry of the child is interpreted as an accusation that she is not as good a mother as she should be, which makes her anxious. And since it was the cry that made her anxious, she interprets it as anxious crying.

This mother shows another type of self-involvement that makes her interpret her child's greater demandingness and frustration not as signs of growth and independence (which they are) but as signs of anger and anxiety. In reality, the anger and the anxiety are in her, but in this particular case they arise less from what actually happens than from what she fears is going to happen in the future.

She does not think to herself, "He needs more of my time now because he's learning more; but this means he will soon be able to do many things by himself." Such a thought would have pleased her and given her added patience for meeting his new demands. Instead she thinks, "These demands are going to increase indefinitely," which makes her anxious. Since she cannot see that her own fear of the future, rather than the child's crying, is what is making her anxious, she again hears it as anxious crying. In reality, he cries out of frustration—because now that he can do more, he still cannot do all he would like to.

That his mother had an unrealistic picture of the glories of motherhood is suggested by her remark that she gets tired of this beautiful life. And on the surface she seems ready to give up her romantic notions of how purely blissful it is to take care of an infant. But she still cannot feel she is successful as a mother if the child whines a lot.

Yet the child who is thus able to threaten the mother's self-image appears to act like (or to be) a little monster. Nowadays many parents, particularly those much concerned with being good parents, seem unable to recognize that they have invested their small children with this power to judge them. Had this mother not invested her son with the power to prove, through his behavior, that she is a good or bad mother, she could have been much more casual about the new developments, including the added crying.

If she could have seen where her irritations came from—her exaggerated notions of how "beautiful" it is to have a small child; her worries about whether she was being a good mother or not—she would have felt no irritation with her child, or only in passing. She would also have been less irritated with herself, and hence able to take pride in her child's developing independence. Because that, after all, proves she was being a good mother.

2

Tyrannized

DR. B.: Are we still talking about spoiling? What do you mean by spoiling?

MOTHER: Mine's spoiled rotten. But he's not being spoiled, any more!

DR. B.: Who am I to argue in favor of your child? I may in a moment, but first tell me your story.

MOTHER: Oh, it's just that I have to be doing something for him all the time!

DR. B.: How old?

MOTHER: He's four.

[*Burst of laughter*]

DR. B.: And when did this tyranny begin?

MOTHER: Right after birth.

DR. B.: How come? Why?

MOTHER: I don't know why. I'm just always waiting on him.

DR. B.: I don't know . . . how serious are you? Are you making this up?

MOTHER: Oh, I'm serious!

DR. B.: All right, then let's talk seriously about it. What does he do that gets you down?

MOTHER: Oh, you've just got to play with him all day long.

DR. B.: So what do you do? Entertain him?

MOTHER: Yes. After all, I want him to be happy.

DR. B.: "By golly, he's going to be happy if it kills me!"

MOTHER: Well ... he's not any more trouble than a two-month-old baby.

DR. B.: Now look, let's not go comparing the different ages; they all have their troubles. The question is, do you have a problem, or do you just want to cry on our shoulders? We'll be happy to provide you with shoulders, but if you want to find out if there's anything you can do about it, then let's talk about it a little more reasonably. Does he go to nursery school? What about it? Isn't there one for the children of veterans on campus?

MOTHER: Well, I have tried. I've waited four or five months to get into that one, but there's a long waiting list.

DR. B.: What about other children on the block?

MOTHER: Oh, he plays with them.

DR. B.: Then he can't be on your hands all the time. What about inviting other children to the house, or boarding him out for a couple of hours?

MOTHER: Other children do come over. But then he's still on my hands. After all, in a small place you can't just let them take over. When it's that small, they're just at your heels all the time.

DR. B.: Well, where else do you want him to be? After all, he has to do something. He's alive. He cannot yet read the Great Books!

MOTHER: No, but before Christmas he would play around the house and he could entertain himself for hours. He was very quiet and very happy.

DR. B.: Who told you he was happy?

MOTHER: Well, he seemed to be. He wasn't demanding; he wasn't crying.

DR. B.: That's right. The mother is ignored and that's identical with the child being happy. Isn't that a funny kind of attitude? [*Turning*] Yes?

SECOND MOTHER: My child is just beginning to walk

and he's just gotten to the stage where he wants me around all the time. But I have the feeling he needs me, that he needs somebody there to reassure him and help him. So I just try to use the free time I have when he sleeps for doing things around the house. Then when he's awake I'll have nothing else on my mind but being a companion to him. I've told my husband, too. That's just the way it's got to be till he's old enough. And in a way . . . things get done haphazardly, but we don't mind.

DR. B.: Good. My point is that what counts is the attitude of the parents. The same child's behavior can be described as "He's happy by himself," or "He ignores me," or "He has no use for me," or "He rejects me." But it can also be described as "He really needs me now," or "I can be of real use to him, and have a chance to teach him," or "He doesn't give me any peace." Now, it's up to you how you interpret the child's behavior to yourself.

SECOND MOTHER: Well, one thing you said last spring helped me a great deal.

DR. B.: You still remember it?

SECOND MOTHER: Oh, yes! It was when you were talking about getting things done . . . how you couldn't do this, and you couldn't do that. You said, "Well, if you have to eat a sandwich, you have to eat a sandwich," and I've really gotten down to that!

[*Burst of laughter*]

DR. B.: And did your husband get down to it?

SECOND MOTHER: He sure did!

DR. B.: The great success of my life! No, I mean it! I'm very happy about it.

SECOND MOTHER: I had so much trouble with the hot stove. I couldn't keep the baby away from it. It just made more trouble for me and for him. And though at first I did try to cook every day, I felt uneasy.

DR. B.: You felt guilty about bawling your child out.

SECOND MOTHER: Yes, I did; but then I resorted to cans and sandwiches. I figure this is just a passing stage, and sooner or later I'll be able to use the stove again.

DR. B.: And sandwiches are cheaper than steaks.

SECOND MOTHER: Anyway, it works. And now if the baby's awake, we eat sandwiches. And if we're hungry by ten at night, then we have something that takes a little longer to cook. That's all you can do!

DR. B.: And you and your husband don't feel sacrificed?

SECOND MOTHER: No, we don't. Sometimes I think if you can just stop worrying about the inanimate things that have to be done, you get much more pleasure out of the kids.

DR. B.: [*turning to mother*] Well, what do you say to that?

MOTHER: Maybe she just has a husband who takes a little different attitude about this.

DR. B.: Maybe, but husbands have to be educated too, just like the children.

MOTHER: Only they take a little longer to come around.

DR. B.: Exactly! Because men are naturally dumb; but why don't you try to teach him?

MOTHER: Okay, I'll try.

DR. B.: Look ... never again in your life will you be so important to a human being. And if you don't enjoy that, you're sunk.

SECOND MOTHER: *My* conclusion was to spend as much time outside the house as I could, with the baby in the carriage. I figure if I can't see these things around the house, I'll forget about them and enjoy myself with the baby.

DR. B.: Well ... there's something else, too. In a way, these problems are typical at midwinter. This is my fourth year of these meetings, and this type of problem always comes up in January. Because it's true; you have to live with the child in the climate of the prefabs, in a very small place. You can take it, and you take it fairly well for a couple of weeks, or a few months. Then comes January and you've had rain and nasty weather and so on, which makes it even harder to get out with small children. It's very unpleasant for them. There's also been sickness, some flu, and it wears mommy down. By now we get low. But I think that as soon as we get nice weather again, you'll be able to get out a little more. Particularly when spring comes, I think you'll see these things ease up. So don't get too desperate. A lot of it is just Chicago in winter.

THIRD MOTHER: Well, but isn't it kind of hard to bring husbands around to accepting these things?

DR. B.: Don't tell me about husbands! I know all about them.

THIRD MOTHER: I had the same trouble . . . fussing at my husband. We used to fight and fight about it. One time I got really mad at him and said, "Now, listen here . . . we've got the baby . . . and we've got to do what we can for her!"

DR. B.: You mean that's the way you talk to him when you're really mad?

THIRD MOTHER: Well, no, I didn't talk quite that way. I was really mad. I don't often lose my temper, but this time I really did. I mean . . . he'd just brought me a bunch of socks, complaining, "Why aren't these mended!" and it was just the last straw. But now that the baby's more of a person, more human, he realizes that a lot of things he wants done can't be done. It took him a long time . . .

DR. B.: Yes . . . I think it's a very serious problem. It's very easy to think about the child. But it's very hard to foresee what it really means . . . in changing your life . . . in changing your relations. It ain't easy, and I think you do very well at a difficult time in your lives.

But to come back to where we started: it was the extra work, the husband's demands, the bad weather that got you down, and that's only natural. It wasn't the child getting spoiled, or that he tyrannized you. And if you can see it for what it is, temporary battle fatigue, everything will soon be okay. But if you see it as your kid tyrannizing you, then it won't be over soon, and it may even get worse. Or, to put it differently—if they get cranky because they're cooped up, we can't expect them to keep up their courage. But if *we* do, they'll do it eventually, too.

3

You Can't Cheat

MOTHER: My little girl is eight months old ...

DR. B.: And she doesn't sleep all night?

MOTHER: No ... but ... what can you do to play with a child that age? I'm bored stiff. I know I shouldn't be, but I am. I'm just bored.

DR. B.: Well, I think it's wonderful that you dare to admit it to yourself. But isn't there anything she does? How much can she do now?

MOTHER: Oh, she pattycakes and I pattycake until I'm blue in the face.

DR. B.: What about singing? Are you good at singing?

MOTHER: No, but I sing to her a lot.

DR. B.: Fine. Well, what else are you good at?

MOTHER: Nothing.

[*Sounds of laughter*]

DR. B.: Oh, come now. Looking for compliments?

MOTHER: Oh, no!

DR. B.: [*Turning*] Who else knows the baby?

MOTHER: Nobody else here.

DR. B.: Well, you should get acquainted; that might help. Eight-month-old babies can be put together in a playpen. Oh sure, they pull hair and there's all kinds of excitement, but ...

SECOND MOTHER: It's not boring!

DR. B.: That's right. It's not boring.

SECOND MOTHER: May I suggest something? Import a neighbor's child. I import my neighbor's boy quite regularly, because . . . well . . . he plays outside the playpen and Mike plays in the playpen, and watches.

DR. B.: Fascinated watching for two full minutes!

SECOND MOTHER: Well, no. My son's very happy as long as there are other children around.

DR. B.: That's right. There's no toy or anything that can entertain like some neighbor children. Well, what about it? Are there any you can import?

MOTHER: Oh! She's entertained enough for part of the time! It's when *I* play with her, that I'm bored. You know, they say one should play with one's child. And I know I shouldn't be bored with her; it's just that she's so stupid! She's awfully stupid, she doesn't . . .

DR. B.: What's the evidence for that?

MOTHER: Well, for instance . . . we played together the other day. I sat down and turned on the light, and she remembers the light for that long. And then the next day she didn't remember anything about it.

SECOND MOTHER: Well, after all, she's only eight months old!

MOTHER: I know, I know! She's only stupid at eight months because at eight months they're all stupid!

SECOND MOTHER: But they're fascinating! Every day they're doing something different, for heaven's sake!

DR. B.: Go ahead; tell us. What do they do?

SECOND MOTHER: Well, they try so hard, and they're so ambitious. Every day they're opening up to some new kind of comprehension. Even the way they hold a cup is different from one day to the next. Any tiny thing!

MOTHER: I taught children at nursery school for two-year-olds, and I think *they*'re interesting. But at eight months they're stupid!

DR. B.: You're just spoiled by your nursery school teaching, that's all.

MOTHER: I suppose so. I know you should like children at that age, but . . .

DR. B.: Oh, don't give me that "should" stuff.

MOTHER: Haven't you known of anybody who thought they were . . . well . . . just dumb?

DR. B.: Well, I'll tell you; I never thought they were geniuses! I grant you, it's very hard to carry on an intelligent conversation with them.

THIRD MOTHER: That I believe.

DR. B.: Why? What's on *your* mind?

THIRD MOTHER: Well, how much does a four-month-old baby really know?

DR. B.: Amazingly much, but in most cases nothing that would relieve the parent's boredom.

THIRD MOTHER: I mean, she looks at you just as if she knows exactly what you're talking about, and what you're thinking about, and as if she's going to answer you any minute.

[*Burst of laughter*]

DR. B.: Go on! Keep talking.

THIRD MOTHER: Well, I think she's interesting . . . but I do get bored staying home, though, all day long.

DR. B.: Well, naturally. Anybody would! [*Turning back to mother.*] How often do you go out?

MOTHER: Oh . . . not very often!

DR. B.: How often have you been to the movies lately?

MOTHER: Three times in the last three months.

DR. B.: Well, don't say it as if you were proud of yourself. You should go out more often. How often have you had company?

MOTHER: Too often . . . maybe too often; all my husband's bachelor friends.

DR. B.: Do you like them all?

MOTHER: Yes . . .

DR. B.: Well ... I don't know. What are you going to do?

THIRD MOTHER: I think she expects too much. Somehow the child is supposed to acquire at birth all the things that the two-year-olds in the nursery school are able to do. But after all, it doesn't happen that fast. It's incredible, the amount they do learn just from week to week at that stage. But they can't jump two years in one fell swoop either.

SECOND MOTHER: I was prepared to be bored with my child until he was two, because I'm interested in two-year-olds, but I'm amazed at how interesting he is!

FOURTH MOTHER: Well, I think we fail to realize the ability of children at that age. I had to have my second one before I realized that my eight-month-old daughter loved the things that my two-year-old son loved to play with.

DR. B.: Yes, but it isn't just the toys, it's the company of your other child. That's why we suggest that she should import other children. Because after everything has been said, the mother obviously doesn't enjoy it very much. She tries to the best of her ability, but she doesn't enjoy it. And if the mother doesn't enjoy it, the child is bored; because the child reacts to the enjoyment of those around him, you know. Just as you describe.

THIRD MOTHER: You can't cheat!

DR. B.: That's right! You cannot cheat! That's true for these small children, and it shows in your imagining that your baby "talks back." It's absolutely amazing how they react ... not to what you say, or what you wish they could do, but what you really feel. And if you're bored, they're bored. It's a vicious circle that you've started, and it's something we have got to break. Do you see what I mean? You are bored, so she is bored, so she's a boring child, so you are bored; and where do we go from there? So we have to make it an interesting child, by awakening some of her interests.

And if you can't do it, let some neighbor children do it.

THIRD MOTHER: Well, I think she's a victim of what a lot of us are. We're stuck at home with the child so much, and it's the only live object on whom she can take out her general boredom and frustration.

DR. B.: No! No! No libels, please. Let's try to help her, not be critical. She's trying her best already by being honest with herself and with us.

THIRD MOTHER: Well, no! I'm not blaming her! I just think that this girl is suffering from the way the world is today. I mean, we don't have help, and baby-sitters are difficult to find. We've got to stay home. We've got all the housework, and all the cooking, and all of everything to do ...

DR. B.: I know! Life is much more boring than before.

THIRD MOTHER: Well, I think she should take up something outside where she'd have a tiny chance of doing something else; where she'd have a chance to get away from the child, if it's remotely possible.

MOTHER: I thought of a job, but ...

DR. B.: That's one solution, and you're the one who knows what will work best for you. But I think if you just give in to it and don't fight it, my girl, you'll be headed for trouble. And it's high time now to do something about it. I can see that if you don't enjoy children and the children are here, it's unfortunate. It's unfortunate for you and unfortunate for the child. Maybe you really want to do something else, and there's the child and you can't. But I still think you have got to make the best of a given situation. If you don't make your daughter welcome now, the trouble will increase as she grows older ... It's up to you ...

While in the first incident ("This Beautiful Life") the mother viewed her child's crying as aggressive and in the second incident the mother felt tyrannized, this mother recognizes that the

245

difficulty did not originate in the child but in her own reaction. True, she makes a half-hearted effort to blame her boredom on the child ("She's so stupid"), but she recognizes that actually the child is only behaving in accordance with its age. Thus it is clear to her all along that things will work themselves out, since she does find children interesting once they are two years old. Any hardship becomes bearable if the end is certain and in sight.

While the first two mothers may eventually endanger their children's views of themselves as worthwhile persons, the worst this third mother's attitude can do is to push her child into developing prematurely. Though it may mean some hardship for the child, it is not likely to be destructive to her.

Since this mother realizes that it is not something in the child, but her own position in society, that is creating the difficulty, this brief incident highlights the problem that young mothers experience nowadays. Her world is no longer, as in an older generation, hard toil to survive the day, nor a world that is confined to child, kitchen, and church. For years, throughout high school and college—and maybe even after college in a professional occupation—she has worked hard to enlarge her horizons, intellectually and emotionally.

Motherhood was depicted to her, and she believed it to be, another tremendous enlarging experience. But actually it forces her to give up most of her old interests. And unless one is fascinated by the minute developments of the infant, as one of the mothers suggests, no new and different enrichment is on the horizon. Thus the new world of experience fails to materialize at the moment when the old enriching experiences are closed because the infant demands the mother's concentrated attention.

All this is particularly acute with the first child, because while she takes care of the second and third, the older child provides content for the mother's life. I am convinced that we shall have to find a solution to this problem. It may come about by creating something akin to the extended family, which in some societies took care of the problem; that is, where part of infant care was entrusted to the older children or shared with relatives. Or it may mean arranging for part-time care of the young child by professional people while the mother pursues her old interests at least part time, be they social or professional in nature. This need is further exemplified by the following incident.

4

A Friendly Solution

MOTHER: I'd like to ask a question. I've been considering having a woman come in for about three hours a day to take my baby out in the buggy; in other words, to take him out. It's interesting that last time you asked who had no problems, and I said I had none. But what was really bothering me was this very thing. I used to paint before the baby came, and I haven't really painted since then except when he was very small. I could sort of see, when he began to stand up, that my even thinking about doing it was out, unless I made some definite arrangements. Before then, I'd have the canvas around anyway. But we only have two rooms and he has one of them. We just live in the other, and I don't know what to do on the days when the weather's bad.

DR. B.: Why couldn't the person you hire stay inside?

MOTHER: Well, inside it's so small, it would just be too crowded.

DR. B.: How old is your son?

MOTHER: He's eight months, and he's still at the stage where he wants to get all over the place. He hasn't really covered the whole house yet, but he branches out more every day.

DR. B.: And you'd like to paint at home?

MOTHER: Yes, that's the thing.

DR. B.: Why do you have to paint at home?

MOTHER: Well, it's really a financial problem. It's hard enough to get a woman, but if I had to get a studio, too, I'd better give up the whole idea for a while. That's what I'm really concerned about. It might be better to decide to forget it till he goes to nursery school, and just let it go at that.

DR. B.: But obviously you're anxious to get back to painting.

MOTHER: Yes, but one thing I was sure of before I ever had him was that I didn't want any conflict. That this was something I could work out; if not during the first two years, then certainly afterward. I just haven't wanted to get into a conflict over it. But obviously something's been going on in my mind, because that was the question I could never ask! I always used to come, planning to ask a question, but everything I could think of always seemed so silly.

DR. B.: Well, it isn't silly at all. Sure, it's your problem, that is, your child has no problem, but unless you solve your own problem, it'll sooner or later rub off on him and then it'll be his problem, too. So it's a real problem, all right: you want to paint.

MOTHER: Everything else seemed silly because I wasn't asking the one thing I really wanted to know.

DR. B.: That's right. It's a real problem if you have such an inclination.

MOTHER: And I was wondering how it would be for him to be closed off. You see, there *is* a porch.

DR. B.: Would it interfere with you if he was crawling around? After all, he doesn't walk yet.

MOTHER: No, but he stands up, and he pulls himself around from one place to another.

DR. B.: Is the easel in danger?

MOTHER: It's a big easel, but of course I could stand it up against the wall so it wouldn't slide. Then there's the matter of grabbing the palette out of the way as fast as possible, so he won't hurt himself.

DR. B.: Do you hold the palette in your hand?

MOTHER: No, it's a big piece of plate glass.

DR. B.: Is that the only way you can paint, with the plate glass?

MOTHER: Yes. I can't hold a palette; I don't work that way.

DR. B.: I see. What about his naps? Why don't you paint when he's napping?

MOTHER: Well, for one thing he doesn't sleep very long. I did do that when he was small. Then when he woke up he'd play in the playpen for a while at my feet, and it didn't disturb me to have him there. But it was very hard to work against this feeling that maybe he'd just sleep an hour instead of two hours, or maybe even a half hour. And then if the telephone bell rings or the delivery man comes, the whole time is shot, you see. Oh, I could do that for a while, but for any length of time I just can't.

DR. B.: It's the hardest age for the mother, there's no doubt.

MOTHER: Yes, and with painting it takes tremendous concentration. I tried to see just how much you could do with interference; I had an idea one could do a lot more than one thought. But when it comes right down to it, it takes concentration.

DR. B.: One always has the idea that children are so nice to have and no trouble at all, but it's just a nice theory. The reality is much different.

MOTHER: Well, I insist that if you can't do both, you might as well . . . I mean . . .

[*Burst of laughter*]

SECOND MOTHER: Would it matter if he were in another room with the other person?

DR. B.: Then, "What is his mother up to?" She isn't doing it as a treat, and he, being a bright child, will know it; even if he were fairly dumb he would know it.

MOTHER: Well, the outing doesn't worry me. The locking him in another room when I'm still there, and he knows it and can't come in, does. If he's entirely out of the house it doesn't seem to matter. I've even considered giving up painting and working at night, writing; because then you don't have to have daylight.

DR. B.: Well, I don't know. I don't have any answer to your problem. I think the child will resent it. If you can wait till nursery school age, it'll solve your problem, of course. In the meantime, I think you'd better take up writing.

MOTHER: You mean, you think he'll resent going out?

DR. B.: No, no. He won't resent that; he resents that he's sent out because you want the time for your painting.

MOTHER: Well, why does he think that? Because he wants the time at home for something?

DR. B.: No, it's very different, but there again you think like an adult. Do you remember, when we discussed one of you girls going out to take a job, and having no qualms about it? That's because her home remained unrestricted.

MOTHER: That's the thing; that's true.

DR. B.: It's not that you want the three hours for yourself. On the contrary, if you want to paint, that's what you should do. What I was getting at when I asked about a studio was that it's enough if you leave him behind with another person. To desert him, so to say, and at the same time restrict him to only one room when he usually has the freedom of the house, that's to be avoided, if possible. One of the two is perfectly all right, but both at the same time might be too much.

MOTHER: You mean, if *I* went out of the house.

DR. B.: If *you* go out, and this woman does a good job, everything is fine.

MOTHER: That's what I mean; he shouldn't be closed off in the house.

DR. B.: That's right. I have no objection if you say, "I want three hours for myself. I want these three hours for my work and I can pay this woman such and such; I can afford it." That's fine. Then the mother doesn't have to become the slave of her child. But if we withdraw the mother, we cannot also withdraw the home.

SECOND MOTHER: Well, Dr. Bettelheim, don't children get used to mothers doing certain things that ... Well, Christine is pretty quiet when I'm on the phone. She's used to it.

[Dissenting groans]

DR. B.: That's because ... I don't know how soon, but the young child realizes that the telephone is an outside interference; that it's not a deliberate act on your part, especially with incoming calls. The telephone rings and obviously there must be somebody you're talking to. The work you do around the house is rarely something you're so concentrated on that you cannot take time out to respond to the child in some way. But this painting business, or writing, or intellectual work so takes you away that any interruption is a bother to you. And if you resist interruptions, not occasionally but always, it's a terribly frustrating experience to a child.

That's why you can do chores around the house, even if there's some irritability and you tell him, "You play there." Because it will only be one out of ten times that you react that way. But with the other kind of work, it'll be nine out of ten times if not ten out of ten. And that gives him the feeling, "There's my mother, and she isn't doing anything sensible. She isn't even preparing food, which I could understand. She's busy with some nonsense."

MOTHER: I agree, it's a mistake to try to do both. I really and truly didn't feel any resentment toward him for interruptions when he was little, and I'd have to go and see to him. But I began to resent my work, because I began to feel it was like dabbling.

DR. B.: Of course. You couldn't concentrate on your work, so it wasn't up to standard.

MOTHER: So it's better to stop it?

DR. B.: No, not to stop it altogether, but to find a good solution to the problem.

SECOND MOTHER: Couldn't you make arrangements for a room at the University; one that's vacant during the hours you want it?

MOTHER: That's what I thought; that something outside would be the only thing.

DR. B.: That's right. Anyhow, you don't restrict him in the home and take away the mother at the same time. Both is too much.

MOTHER: That's what I meant.

This mother is not bored. She knows that what is missing is in her, so she does not need to fight off the realization, nor blame her difficulty on the child. Even more significantly, she has already, on her own, explored various ways of improving the situation, and considered possible alternatives. For example, she has thought of writing instead of painting, which suggests that what she needs is not even painting so much as an activity that satisfies her need.

Her need is to find a fulfillment as a person that is now lacking, despite her clear attachment and devotion to her child. But though she needs the activity, she is willing to compromise with her child as to its nature. Thus she seeks a friendly solution, and because of it there is no head-on clash between her and the child. I might add that nothing eliminates boredom more successfully than engaging in the search for ways to end it. Battle fatigue, too, is best relieved by looking for solutions to what brought on the battle in the first place.

DISCUS BOOKS

DISTINGUISHED NON-FICTION

THEATER, FILM AND TELEVISION

ACTORS TALK ABOUT ACTING Lewis Funke and John Booth, Eds.	15062	1.95
ANTONIN ARTAUD Bettina L. Knapp	12062	1.65
A BOOK ON THE OPEN THEATER Robert Pasoli	12047	1.65
THE CONCISE ENCYCLOPEDIC GUIDE TO SHAKESPEARE Michael Martin and Richard Harrier, Eds.	16832	2.65
THE DISNEY VERSION Richard Schnickel	08953	1.25
EDWARD ALBEE: A PLAYWRIGHT IN PROTEST Michael E. Rutenberg	11916	1.65
THE EMPTY SPACE Peter Brook	32763	1.95
EXPERIMENTAL THEATER James Roose-Evans	11981	1.65
FOUR CENTURIES OF SHAKESPEARIAN CRITICISM Frank Kermode, Ed.	20131	1.95
GUERILLA STREET THEATRE Henry Lesnick, Ed.	15198	2.45
THE HOLLYWOOD SCREENWRITERS Richard Corliss	12450	1.95
IN SEARCH OF LIGHT: THE BROADCASTS OF EDWARD R. MURROW Edward Bliss, Ed.	19372	1.95
INTERVIEWS WITH FILM DIRECTORS Andrew Sarris	21568	1.95
MOVIES FOR KIDS Edith Zornow and Ruth Goldstein	17012	1.65
PICTURE Lillian Ross	08839	1.25
THE LIVING THEATRE Pierre Biner	17640	1.65
PUBLIC DOMAIN Richard Schechner	12104	1.65
RADICAL THEATRE NOTEBOOK Arthur Sainer	22442	2.65
SOMETHING WONDERFUL RIGHT AWAY Jeffrey Sweet	37119	2.95
TO DANCE Valery Panov	47233	3.95

GENERAL NON-FICTION

ADDING A DIMENSION Isaac Asimov	36871	1.50
A TESTAMENT Frank Lloyd Wright	12039	1.65
AMBIGUOUS AFRICA Georges Balandier	25288	2.25
THE AMERICAN CHALLENGE J. J. Servan Schreiber	11965	1.65
AMERICA THE RAPED Gene Marine	09373	1.25
ARE YOU RUNNING WITH ME, JESUS? Malcolm Boyd	09993	1.25
THE AWAKENING OF INTELLIGENCE J. Krishnamurti	45674	3.50
THE BIOGRAPHY OF ALICE B. TOKLAS Linda Simon	39073	2.95
THE BOOK OF IMAGINARY BEINGS Jorge Luis Borges	11080	1.45
BUILDING THE EARTH Pierre de Chardin	08938	1.25
CHEYENNE AUTUMN Mari Sandoz	39255	2.25
THE CHILD IN THE FAMILY Maria Montessori	28118	1.50
THE CHILDREN'S REPUBLIC Edward Mobius	21337	1.50
CHINA: SCIENCE WALKS ON TWO LEGS Science for the People	20123	1.75
CLASSICS REVISITED Kenneth Rexroth	08920	1.25

(1) DDB 11-79

DISCUS BOOKS

DISTINGUISHED NON-FICTION

DISCUS BOOKS

DISTINGUISHED NON-FICTION

Wherever better paperbacks are sold, or direct from the publisher. Include 50¢ per copy for postage and handling; allow 4-6 weeks for delivery.

Avon Books, Mail Order Dept.
224 W. 57th St., New York, N.Y. 10019

(3) DDB 11-79